WOMEN
Ready to
RISE

"Jenn Sadai's *Women Ready to Rise* is the pep talk I didn't know that I needed. Sadai is healing women with every book she writes. Her stories give people purpose, experience, and motivation to continue to take stabs at life, because no matter how hard the pain is, they will be ready to rise again. Jenn's books have literally shaped me into the woman I am today. Not only does her writing impact my life in more than one book, but she bases her books off of real people, real experiences, and gives everyone a light in the dark, a light they probably didn't know would ever shine again. I was in a real dark time in my life when I first met Jenn at one of her book launches, while working for a magazine that was covering the event. She was not only stunning, but her presence was comforting. At this point, I didn't know Jenn at all. But then again, I felt as if I already did.

Women Ready to Rise is empowering, thoughtful, and poetic, as my mind has never wandered through so many similar experiences, but with them being so different at the same time. I felt their voices being heard and I felt them rising alongside me. I suffered from suicidal thoughts, depression, extreme anxiety, social anxiety, and attempted to take my own life, but reading experiences like the women in this book has shown me a light I haven't seen in a while. A light I needed to see for myself.

With all this being said, Jenn Sadai made me love life again and made me realize that life is more than wishing you could move on from your past. It's about making your life worth living with the experiences you've fought to be here today."

—CHELSEA GIRARD,
Author of *A Delicate Flower*

ALSO BY JENN SADAI

THE SELF-ESTEEM SERIES
Dark Confessions of an Extraordinary, Ordinary Woman
Dirty Secrets of the World's Worst Employee
Cottage Cheese Thighs

THE SURVIVOR SERIES
Her Own Hero
Her Beauty Burns

TRUE TALES SERIES
No Kids Required
Women Ready to Rise

WOMEN
Ready to
RISE

Jenn Sadai

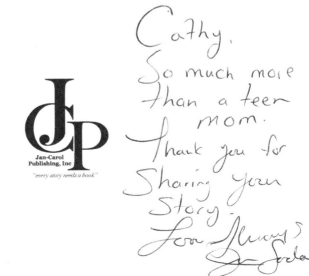

Jan-Carol Publishing, Inc

"every story needs a book"

Cathy,
So much more
than a teen
mom.
Thank you for
Sharing your
Story.
Love Always?
Jenn Sadai

Women Ready to Rise
Jenn Sadai

Published March 2020
Express Editions
Imprint of Jan-Carol Publishing, Inc

ISBN: 978-1-950895-31-1
Library of Congress Control Number: 2020934011

You may contact the publisher:
Jan-Carol Publishing, Inc
PO Box 701
Johnson City, TN 37605
publisher@jancarolpublishing.com
jancarolpublishing.com

This book is dedicated to the 22 brave and resilient women who shared their stories of survival. Thank you Katelynn, Kim, Cathy, Deb, Kimberly, Tina, Lisa, Dana, Kenzie, Sheryl, Rahel, Leonora, Evie, Jenny, Jody, Renee, JJ, Steph, Sandra, Carrie, Stacey, and Natalie for your vulnerability and honesty. You will inspire many.

LETTER TO THE READER

Life will knock you down. It will break your heart and take your breath away. Everyone has moments when it feels like the weight of the world is crushing you. Hopelessness forces its way in and you feel like you will never rise again.

Women Ready to Rise is proof that you can and will survive.

I interviewed twenty-two women who have endured the worst the world has to offer and found a way to keep moving forward. These women overcame immense obstacles such as the tragic loss of a loved one, teenage pregnancy, physical and emotional abuse, sexual assault and rape, bone-breaking bullying, sudden job loss, raising a severely disabled child, and serious health concerns, including depression, anxiety, vision impairment, and breast cancer. Many of these women wanted to give up and a few even attempted to end their life before finally seeing the light at the end of the tunnel.

Twenty-two brave women are sharing their deeply personal stories to inspire you not to give up. There is always hope; life can and will get better. These extraordinary, yet ordinary women rose again and so will you.

With love always,

Jenn Sadai

FOREWORD

By Stephanie Renaud

Everyone struggles.

Everyone falls.

The trouble, I find, is that so many people consider their struggles and failures to be evidence of their unworthiness. I know I did for a long time. And yet, we all have heroes. People that we look to and think that if we could just be like them, life would be better. Or maybe we think we could never be like them, that we are too flawed or broken or unexceptional to stand in their shoes.

We admire their courage, their strength, their resolve in the face of insurmountable odds. To our eyes they are exceptional, and born with a heroic destiny, so very unlike our own. But what if we were wrong?

What if it is our struggles that define us? What if every dark night we have experienced and risen from is what makes us who we are? What if the exceptional courage that our heroes embody is available to all of us in our own darkest moments? And what if it's the story we tell ourselves about ourselves that determines whether the cruelties of life crush us or create us?

Between the pages of this book you will find stories of heroic women, women who have been abandoned, assaulted, abused, lost children, lost marriages, lived with disability, struggled with addiction, and you may find yourself thinking that you could never be like them. You would never have the courage to face and conquer their odds. They are, after all, heroes, or they wouldn't be in this book.

I invite you to look within yourself, and see the hero that is you. You too are a woman ready to rise. Maybe you haven't yet, but you have it in you to join the ranks of these women. In fact, I would wager that you are already ready. You just don't know it yet.

Your hero story starts with your next choice.

Stephanie Renaud, **Author of** The Courage Key: How to Unlock Yourself from Anxiety & Take Back Control

WOMEN READY TO RISE

W hat is a woman ready to rise?

My initial concept, which grew into this collection of powerful stories, merely meant these women were ready to rise when life tried to knock them down. That was my idea, and the intention behind the title.

Somehow, those four little words were powerful enough to intimidate several candidates out of participating in this story, and turned one wonderful woman off of my purpose completely. Some women I asked didn't feel they had truly risen from their challenges (even after I enthusiastically insisted that they had); one felt the title implied she hadn't already risen. Each woman interprets those four words based on her own mindset.

Perception plays a critical role in how we live our lives and the choices we make. How we perceive ourselves, how we view others, how we interpret a situation, and the way we react are all based on our thought processes. Our minds control our response.

When we think we're not worthy or we're not capable of doing something, we're not as committed to our success. We don't put in the required effort to achieve what we believe is unattainable. We let doubts dictate our decisions, or we allow fear to stop us from even trying. What we perceive to be often becomes our reality.

I want this book to convince you that you're worthy and more capable than you realize. Every woman I know is a woman ready to rise; that innate power to survive exists in every soul. Anyone who has faced a time in their life when it would have been easier to give up than it would be to push forward, then chose to keep going, fits my interpretation of those four words. Life will continuously throw challenges in front of you. A woman ready to rise will always find a way to bust through, regardless of the roadblock.

I didn't know I was a woman ready to rise until long after I had risen from my past and created this wonderfully crazy life I'm living now. I also didn't realize that I am merely one of millions and millions of determined women who have found a way to move forward in spite of an avalanche of obstacles, setbacks, and internal devastation.

I'm an author who believes that everyone has a story. When I wrote my first book, detailing my less-than-perfect childhood and far-from-healthy romantic relationship, I had no idea how many women would actually relate to my experiences. I thought my story was exceptionally tragic; instead, I discovered it was rather mild in comparison to countless others.

It broke my heart to learn that all of these women were secretly trying to heal from similar pain. They were too frightened, embarrassed, insecure, and unsure to admit what they endured at the hands of someone they loved until they saw someone else with the courage to speak up. Some were still stuck in toxic relationships, and my story hit them like a ton of bricks. Just by reading how far I fell before I rose again, gave several women the courage to finally break free.

My voice empowered theirs.

The heart-bursting feeling of helping and encouraging others is the single strongest motivator for me as a writer. My goal with this book is to share that life-changing power with the numerous other warrior women whom I interviewed, while using their powerful stories of survival to inspire the best in anyone who reads it.

Through my networking and advocacy efforts, I've met an astounding number of impressive women over the past few years. The greatest challenge writing this story was deciding which of these women best represented a woman ready to rise. You'll notice I snuck in a few extra stories about other women throughout the book, because everybody has risen from something.

Every woman has an inspiring story worth sharing, whether I included it or not. Selecting which women should be featured was a two-year process filled with excitement, disappointment, and occasionally second-guessing myself. My list of women was fluid up until the final copy was sent to the printer. Several ideal candidates didn't have either the time or desire to put their personal lives in print; some found it too emotional to retell (relive) their most painful memories, and some were intimidated or felt unworthy.

We are *all* worthy.

There were no wrong choices, only some extraordinary women who felt exceptionally right. I specifically chose diverse women with varied histories, so that every reader can find something that relates to their own experiences. Realizing we're not alone, and that others have felt the same way, truly helps us heal.

I am honored these 22 women agreed to let me tell their tales of turning tragedies into triumphs. Each chapter in this book will delve into two women's personal stories of surviving shocking struggles and how they used the strength it gave them to become the best version of themselves. These pages are flooded with evidence proving women can handle anything.

I want their stories to give you hope that you, too, can overcome whatever is holding you down. We have the resilience to heal from even the heaviest of heartaches. I'm amazed by the number of women who have faced days darker than I've ever seen, yet are now shining so brightly they warm my soul. They are proof that you can not only survive immense pain, you can also learn to thrive again. No matter what happens, or how low you sink, you have the ability to rise again.

I need this reminder every so often as well. Although my life is finally on a more joyful path, it has its share of bumps. I still have messy moments and painful heartbreak. I put myself out there in a flashy fashion, which occasionally results in harsh backlash. I've exposed my abusive ex and a former boss's dirty deeds in my first memoirs, putting me at risk for retaliation.

When sales drop off or I receive a bad review, the urge to throw in the towel occasionally creeps in, at least as far as my writing career goes.

It doesn't happen very often anymore, and thankfully, I have discovered the magical solution for when it does.

I connect with other stubbornly successful authors and enthusiastic entrepreneurs. Bearing witness to their ambition and determination gives me the boost I need to bounce back up. Unbeknownst to them, the women in this book lift me up every time I fall. Genuine inspiration.

That's how life is meant to work. We're on this earth together to support and encourage one another, not to suffer alone. If you are brave enough to be open and honest about your feelings when you'd rather just shut down and hide, there's usually someone willing to offer assistance, or at least listen with compassion. Sometimes simply knowing that someone else cares is enough to keep you going, inspiring hope.

Those who were helped back up, when they were at their personal rock bottom, develop this overwhelming urge to pay it forward. Kindness spreads to those impacted by it, but it becomes an unstoppable force when it blossoms from helping someone get through the moments they thought they'd never survive. Family and friends helped me rise when I hit rock bottom. I share my story and reach out to those in need, so I can lift others off the ground. Once risen, they reach back down to raise someone else from despair. Contagious inspiration.

It's a cycle our world needs to grow, especially for women. In spite of our proclaimed equality, women are still significantly more likely to be abused or raped. Many of the stories you're about to read showcase resilient women rising above evil men. Men control the majority of the money and the power in our current world; that's the cold, hard facts. Women need to gain more influential roles and make significant capital gains, so that we have the leverage to fight back against the men who attempt to oppress us. We rise higher by working together.

Women are so much stronger than they realize. The 22 fierce women you're about to meet all went through something beyond their control that turned their world upside down. They were faced with giving up or pushing forward. A little nudge in the right direction from someone in their life, maybe several people, guided them back on track.

They faced some of the greatest challenges imaginable and found a way to power through. Now they are sharing everything they've endured and achieved, to show you that you can do it too. No matter what happens in life, there is always hope it will get better. When you're finished reading this story, please keep the cycle going.

Your story matters too.

GOOD GRACIOUS GRIEF

My first woman ready to rise was introduced to me as being an ideal candidate for this book by a lovely, empowered woman whom I already trusted. I posted my *Women Ready to Rise* concept on social media in a search of the most courageous and compassionate women, and the founder of a local women's support group (and fantastic friend) immediately suggested Katelynn.

> "Hey there! I agree everyone has a story of struggle and how they overcome it. It's incredible! There is a lady who lost her daughter at 17 months, and also went through ovarian cancer at 27. She is a light. When you meet her, you just know she's special before you even hear her story. Her name is Katelynn."

I've now met Katelynn several times, and know exactly what Jessica meant by the light that shines through her. I follow her self-esteem boosting posts on social media, and she beams in her pictures in a way that you would assume her entire life was bliss. No one who looks that happy could have experienced such loss and tragedy, you'd think.

Katelynn can. Her smile bursts from her cheeks as if she had every reason to celebrate, yet her life has never been easy. She's survived more than most people could fathom, far beyond Jessica's initial synopsis. Good gracious grief, Katelynn's had to find her way back up countless times and continues to rise.

I doubt she realizes just how remarkable the obstacles she has overcome sound to the rest of us. When asked why she thought I chose her for this story, she humbly responded, "I've had huge life experiences, which have shaped me into the woman I am today and the woman I am becoming. I aim to inspire women by sharing my life experiences, spreading hope and a positive attitude."

Katelynn refers to so much loss and pain as "huge life experiences," and already knows she has the power to inspire others. The hardest moments in our life will inevitably shape who we become. If you lose all hope and fall into the negativity, that's the life you will attract. If you find the will to keep going and search for a bright side, you gain the strength to rise above it. Katelynn knows this to be true because she's lived through it, time and time again.

"I was raised in foster care, fourteen placements to be exact, all of which have shaped the badass mom and human I am today. During my upbringing, I endured physical abuse, emotional abuse, abandonment, suicide attempts, rape, a house fire, and finally drug and alcohol abuse."

Katelynn lists the extreme challenges that have plagued her life as if they were ordinary obstacles that every person was expected to experience. I noticed she missed mentioning the ovarian cancer Jessica referenced in the introduction. When I inquired about it, Katelynn brushed it off as no big deal, because they caught it early enough to avoid chemotherapy.

When you've been through so much tragedy, something easily treatable isn't that scary, even when it's attached to the dreaded six-letter word *cancer*. For Katelynn, it was motivation to promote safe, natural beauty products, her current, passion-filled career.

A tested survivor, she sought out the good that could come from her cancer. Katelynn grew up without stability, structure, or a place to call home, so she learned how to reassure herself that she'd make it through whatever trauma happened next. It's awe-inspiring that Katelynn sees how everything her childhood lacked ending up giving her exactly what she needed.

"There is one story from my foster care experiences that I love. My last foster home, Mom and I went to see a movie together: *The Butterfly Effect*. I was around fourteen or fifteen when this movie came out. As you can imagine, if you've seen it, the movie really made me think about my own life.

"As we were leaving the theatre, my foster mom said to me 'So, Katie, how do you feel about that show? Do you wish you could make your outcome different?' I thought about it for a second, looked at her, and said 'Not really, because then I wouldn't have had you in my life.'

"This small moment in my life has stayed with me and my mom; it still rings true today. I wouldn't change anything, no matter how awful and how much suffering I had. There would be a butterfly effect of change to follow any one change to my past. I'm not willing to take that chance."

It's heartbreaking that someone so positive and caring had to endure so much to become the person she is today, but every struggle makes us stronger. An unstable and abuse-filled childhood made her resilient and experienced at handling trauma, which would be a necessary skill for her next heartbreak.

"For most of my life, I have been in survival mode. As a child, I never thought anyone loved me or cared for my well-being."

Katelynn met her husband at the age of eighteen, and for the first time, she truly understood the power of real love. He gave her the desperately needed unconditional acceptance and encouragement that was missing from her upbringing and saw the best in her, despite her soul being wrought with tragedy.

It was time for Katelynn to have the normal, stable life she deserved. They married and had a son, Benjamin, beginning the family she always dreamt she would have one day. Katelynn felt alive! Being a devoted mom quickly turned into her greatest purpose in life.

Eager to add to their loving family, Katelynn became pregnant again, only to end up suffering a miscarriage at sixteen weeks. It broke their hearts, but couldn't break their spirits. Considering the childhood Katelynn survived, it's obvious she is not one who will give up easily. They wanted a girl, and soon tried again for the daughter they desperately wanted. Their dreams came true when their daughter Jocelynn was born, completing the family she had pictured when she was being shuffled from foster home to foster home. In Katelynn's words:

> "My life was complete. I was fulfilled being a mom and raising my children with so much love and happiness, everything I never had as a child. There was nothing else I needed or wanted in life."

There was nothing else she could ask of her life. The love she'd been missing when young was abundant and thriving with her husband and two children. I wish I could end Katelynn's story right here, but as you know from Jessica's introduction to me, there's far more heartache scattered along her journey.

> "This perfect life I created came to a sudden end when I found my seventeen-month-old daughter in her crib one morning, lifeless. My whole world stopped. My heart shattered. I felt the worst pain any human can feel. I lost my child forever."

Every mother, and most likely every person, reading this book can't see through their tears at the moment. I've read it so many times through the editing process, and I still cry. Losing a child is a pain no parent thinks they will ever find a way to get past, but somehow, so many do. Tragic moments of grief in our lives force us to either bury ourselves with the dead, or push ourselves to rise above.

> "After Jocelynn passed away, I immediately went on a search for help. I knew I couldn't handle this loss alone. I needed support in order to be a good mom to Benjamin. Instead of falling into old

habits of drugs and alcohol, I leaned on the community support and reached out to people. I still wanted to be a great mother to my oldest child."

Katelynn started grief counseling with her husband right after their daughter's death, and knows that was the best decision they could have made. The week following Jocelynn's passing, they began the long, challenging process of working through the shock, terror, and pain. Knowing she needed to be there for her son Benjamin kept her going during times when the pain of losing Jocelynn was unbearable.

"The loss of a child...I will never overcome it. I have learned to honor my loss and my grief. She is very much a part of our daily lives, and her spirit lives on."

They did decide to try again a year later and were blessed with another boy, named Emmett. He was the final piece their family needed to heal their broken heart. Although Jocelynn lives on inside their hearts and can never be replaced, Emmett taught her family how to love again.

Katelynn counts her blessings and acknowledges the power of forgiveness. She recognizes how searching for a positive perspective during dark times helps her move forward. Forgiving her mother and those who harmed her in the past was essential to her healing. She has found purpose for her pain, easing the weight it places on her heart.

"I would not be who I am today if I didn't go through what I went through, because I have compassion, drive, and life knowledge because of it. My childhood was extremely difficult, but it made me a mindful parent. I'm more in tune with my kids' needs.

"I'm a better person. I am kind, I don't pass judgment. I try to see the good in everyone. I'm always willing to help others and go out of my way. This is because growing up, I had people who did this for me. I had kids give me food when I had nothing, I had adults show me love when I was dirty and smelly from neglect.

Compassion goes a long way and I'm happy I learned that. Losing my daughter has given me the drive to help other women who have lost their children. I offer support in any way I can."

Katelynn is an online advocate and sales representative for safer cosmetics and consumer products, which has built quite a significant following. She uses her reach to openly discuss mental health issues, unrealistic beauty standards, and dealing with tragic grief. Her body-positive posts, showing that we are all fabulously flawed, lift me and so many others.

Katelynn is very real and candid about how her experiences have shaped the person she is today, because she knows her voice has power. She remembers when she felt lost, numb, and worthless. At her lowest point, Katelynn wanted to end her life. Now, she shares herself with the world to help grieving parents know they can live through it.

Katelynn's followers see her as a positive influence who's always happy, even though she openly admits to her struggles with grief, parenting, and self-esteem. She credits mediation, yoga, and mindfulness practice as her methods for rising above any negativity that tries to penetrate her self-confidence.

"It's a constant battle. I always have to remind myself that I'm worthy, I am amazing, and I can do anything I put my mind to, even though it's hard at times. I have to push through. Mindfulness practice has been a savior in my adulthood.

"I've had many role models in my life. I've lived with women who stayed home, women who had careers, and women who took care of farms. Each one had unique strengths that I admire, such as hard work, dedication, compassion, and love.

"After my daughter passed away, my son was the only person keeping me going. I wanted to give up; I even wanted to die myself. He kept the light shining in my heart. He inspired me to play, love and see the beauty in life. The women I met along the way inspired me at my lowest point; I had their voices encouraging me forward."

Now Katelynn is allowing me to share her story with you to encourage you to move forward, no matter what happens. There is always a way to keep going. I can't imagine losing a child. Anyone who hasn't been through it still knows it's an unthinkable nightmare of epic portions, and that's not all Katelynn has had to overcome in life. Her resilience and ability to move forward and become a shining example of a rising star, is proof that there is always hope for a better tomorrow.

I've lost a few people I loved: three grandparents, the uncle who inspired me to write, and a warm and vibrant woman who was this beautiful combination of mother and friend to me. I struggled to process that last loss in particular, because as much as it created a void in my life, it blew apart someone I love dearly, along with an entire family of truly good people. Death devastated their world for the second time, and the story of that itself is beyond tragic. I couldn't even process the pain they must have felt, for mine was minor in comparison, yet still soul-shattering.

Grief is wicked. Over the past few years, I've watched it darken one of the brightest shining spirits I know. She digs deep to find the energy and positive outlook to keep going, but her heart has been broken into tiny pieces more than once. Kim was the first person who came to mind when I had the idea for this story. She is my main inspiration for this book (and so many other aspects of my life), yet she was the one who felt the least worthy.

It took several borderline harassing emails and cajoling, convincing conversations to provoke her participation. I finally received Kim's answers a year later, after we spent a weekend together connecting with a group of brilliantly resilient women. We spent two days sharing our joys and heartaches freely, without fear or judgment. I think that was the nudge Kim needed to write out the thoughts consuming her heart.

"I don't feel like I'm rising. I'm still struggling. I'm still hurting. The pain and grief of losing my mom, who was also my best friend, is still hard for me to deal with on a regular basis. I thought my mom would be with me till she was in her late eighties at least, maybe late nineties. She was the healthiest person I know. I would be old by then. She should have lived the longest life. But the good die young, right? A giant piece of my heart is missing, and I'll never be the same without her."

Kim is still struggling, and that's OK. Her life has been a roller coaster of fantastic highs and dramatic lows, and it's not suddenly perfect just because I'm calling her a woman ready to rise. She is still climbing her way back up. Kim has tragically lost so many people in her life that it is unbelievably unfair. It feels exceptionally cruel to me, as someone who has watched her and her family face funeral after funeral. The heartache of their reality affects everyone who loves their family.

Although chunks of her heart were torn out, Kim has found a way to continue thriving. She's a mother of two confident, talented twin boys, a highly motivating fitness trainer, and a phenomenal graphic design artist (my personal book cover designer). She is so much fun to be around, and a loyal friend to anyone who needs her. She's a warm ball of energy, like the sun.

Kim lost a good childhood friend, followed by her sister, grandma, and mother, all well before their time. Four female figures, taken too soon. Can you imagine having a fourth person you love stolen from you without warning, and weeks later, cheering on people to improve their health so they can live longer?

Kim can. She inspires people to take care of themselves, while struggling to find her own will to keep going. Every day she gathers the strength not only to pull herself out of bed, she somehow finds the ability to lift those around her throughout the day. She's my hero. Just by rising every morning, she inspires me to push through the hard moments in my own life. Kim uses her sorrows as a reason to live a full, vibrant life.

"Losing so many people close to me, far too young and unexpectedly, has taught me to cherish every moment. Life is short. You hear those words all the time, but it's so true. Losing my sister, a close friend, a grandma, and then my mom unexpectedly, well... you never know. I am very much surrounded by love and I am extremely grateful for that every day."

Although she's lost so many people that she deeply loved, she's most grateful for still being surrounded by so many people who truly love her. Kim counts her blessings. That is how she's powered through so many heartbreaking moments.

Kim was blessed with a welcoming, involved, and loving family. They made me feel like I was a part of the family from day one. Her dad's infectious sense of humor gives you gut-bursting laughs, and her mother was the trusted confidante that anyone could go to for advice. Those are traits Kim inherited. It amazes me that they are still so full of life after experiencing so much death.

Her first painful loss was on the brink of adulthood, when her sister Melanie made a fatal mistake. She had a couple drinks at a party and was driving Kim's close friend home when Melanie fell asleep at the wheel. The car hit a median and flipped.

There were three young, promising teenagers in the car that day, and one did not survive the crash. She was not over the legal limit. However, due to being under the legal age to drink and having any alcohol in her system, the incident was treated as if it was a drunk driving accident. A split-second mistake, possibly not even within her control, branded Melanie and her family as a cautionary tale.

Dealing with the anger of losing a good friend under such tragic circumstances, accompanied with her sister becoming the hot topic in their small-town community, was a lot for Kim to absorb when she was a teenager transitioning into an adult.

Maybe that's why she rushed into marrying a man who was never good enough for her when she was still so young.

Kim's desire to seize every moment and move on with life may have been why she settled for her high school sweetheart, marrying him when she was only 23. He was an seemingly-decent guy who treated her fine in the beginning, but his love of alcohol and drugs superseded his love for her. When tragedy struck Kim's life for the second time, he was useless.

I must admit, that's my personal opinion of her thankfully now *ex*-husband. As someone who has spent a fair amount of time with the family when her sister Melanie was suddenly ripped from this earth, I noticed how her ex would always disappear when she needed him the most. My opinion and frustration comes from repeated exposure to "men" (greedy, selfish, oversized boys) who choose themselves over everyone else.

Several years later, Kim's 24-year-old sister was sober, driving home at night, and blacked out again—possibly as a result of injuries she endured during the first accident. Their family had finally healed and moved on from the first tragic accident. Melanie passed away in the crash and now she was permanently gone under similar circumstances.

With time, they were able to celebrate Melanie's life rather than allowing her death to swallow their lives.

> "When Melanie passed away, she had just started her teaching career and was working two teaching jobs. To honor her life, we put together a fun winery tour and silent auction to build a scholarship for aspiring teachers. Every year, the university chooses one student who is given a $1,000 grant in Melanie's name. We receive letters thanking us from the teachers, and that keeps Melanie's spirit alive."

I found it physically painful to watch her tightly-knit family mourn such a devastation. However, they handled it better than I did. They quickly found a purpose for the pain, and used their loss as a catalyst to give back. Although her family rebounded from the heartbreak and found a way to move forward, losing your baby sister is life-shattering, and the man closest to Kim only amplified her struggles.

Kim had young twins and despite the obvious flaws in her husband, it took her several years to work up the courage to leave him. As a dependent, miserable man, he did not take the news very well. Her ex made everything harder than it needed to be, and his criminal activities escalated. It is now over eight years later and he still doesn't help enough with the financial aspect of raising two young men.

As life has a way of giving us what we need, Kim met a man worthy of her love, shortly after leaving her husband. Her second (and I'm predicting final) romance is with a young, energetic, kindhearted man who knows how lucky he is to be with her. Her face glows when she's with him.

Rick was definitely there for her when the matriarch of their family suddenly passed, despite being extraordinarily active for her age. All grandmothers and grandfathers eventually pass on, however that loss should never be quickly followed by losing a mother who was only 59 years old.

> "When Mel passed away, it was different. I had these little twin two-year-old boys who were just a joy to be around. I had to care for them, so I didn't have time to feel depressed. I was also in a different relationship and didn't have a person to hold me at night, so I could release those tears. When my mom passed away suddenly, at 59 years old, when we were like best friends, it was just so hard. It was too young, too soon."

Although losing Dawna (a mother to so many) rocked his world as well, Rick was the rock Kim needed when the biggest piece of her heart suddenly slipped away in a second. Her mother was discreetly fighting cancer for a second time, and didn't want those in her world to worry about her. By the time Kim knew the severity, it was too late.

I didn't ask Kim to write about losing Dawna. Her mom is always on her mind, yet I knew writing about what happened or how she felt would be too hard. This happened in the summer of 2017, so the wound is still quite fresh. Dawna was here and then gone in a blink of an eye.

At the beginning of August, Kim knew her mom was having tests and not feeling well. She was supposed to attend a party at my house on the 5th, and cancelled last minute to be with her family. On August 10th, it appeared that her mom would be OK—or at least that was what Kim thought, when I asked.

On August 11th, she was admitted to the hospital with cancer and they set up a treatment plan. By August 12th, she was no longer coherent or responsive, looking like a shell of herself. August 13th, we were broken puddles on the floor of the hospital, praying for a miracle, hugging her desperately and trying to bring life back into her.

On August 14th, surrounded by her children and her husband, Dawna took her last breath.

Writing this book provoked tears that made it hard to type many times, yet nothing was as torrential as this portion. I loved Dawna like a mother, plus she was dearly loved by someone I love like a sister. The immense pain I feel is magnified a thousand times in Kim's eyes when we dare to discuss the subject after a few too many alcoholic beverages.

Kim and I have shared countless emotional, insightful, intimate conversations after enjoying more than our share of alcohol. Booze miraculously doesn't hinder Kim's judgment (she's too smart to do anything foolish), although I think it makes it easier for her to talk about her pain. With her blessing, I recorded our last deep discussion.

"Everyone says to me, 'you're so strong, you're so strong,' but I'm not. I have those moments of weakness when I feel low and unmotivated. I thought the grief would get better with time, but it hasn't, in a way. The longer she's gone, the more of my life she's missing out on. It's never going to be easy; I'll always miss her. It's refreshing to get it out and have that cry.

"You need motivation to focus your mind on other things, so you don't settle into that grief and despair. Doing things to care for yourself, finding ways to feel better about yourself, it is essential to avoid slipping into a depression when you're grieving so hard."

Kim is a social, spiritual, genuine being who embodies the best qualities of both her parents. After losing her sister, she did everything with them, including a weekly house party. I couldn't count how many times we hung out with her folks until the wee hours of the morning. They were so laid back and accepting, eagerly willing to play games or music with anyone who showed up.

"That's why I live my life having the most fun I can, and doing what makes me happy. I appreciate every moment, and the people I love with all my heart. Maybe that's rising...I hope. Things can change in a second. You don't want to be left with any regrets or what-ifs.

"Living and dying is actually a beautiful thing. I used to be afraid of death. But when you see the circle of life, and when love surrounds it... It's truly amazing. That gives me some sort of peace in my heart now."

I believe Kim is a woman ready to rise because she can still see the good in every day. She is grateful to wake up every morning, ready to celebrate life, and lifts everyone she meets as she goes. Knowing Kim has lifted me higher than I thought possible, and I hope her resilience inspires you to rise.

Grief can easily become consuming and you can lose your passion for life in the death of someone you love dearly. It's perfectly normal to take time to grieve, going through the process of denial and anger, allowing yourself a long enough pause to feel sad. Just don't stay there. Find comfort in those still on earth, and cherish the warmest memories of those you can't hold anymore.

TOO YOUNG TO BE A MOM?

Raising children is quite possibly the most difficult task a woman will ever take on. It's a lifelong commitment that requires countless sacrifices. From the body-morphing pregnancy to caring for a totally dependent infant, followed by terrible twos, reckless teenagers, and foolish young adults, every aspect of having a child is terrifying. I wasn't ready in my twenties, and have now completely opted out of the experience because I don't feel selfless enough to do it.

Can you picture making this decision when you're still a child?

My mom was a teenaged mom, the very same age as the next risen woman, and their stories are somewhat similar. I saw everything my mom gave up in exchange for my brother and me; it's a hard way to start out your life. One of my oldest friends, whom I'll officially introduce in the second half of this chapter, had two kids under the age of two when we were in college. Although she eventually found a way to succeed, the additional responsibility hindered her progress at every step.

Cathy is another wonderful example of a woman ready to rise, because she understands just how hard it is to be a teen mom. She was only fifteen years old when she had to decide if she was ready to accept the full-time role of motherhood. To make it more difficult, she didn't have a family capable of supporting her. Cathy's own parents were miserable, verbally abusive, and too poor to help her financially.

In her first year of high school, Cathy made the decision to have sex with her boyfriend after they had been together for three months. She was educated and knew to go on birth control two months prior to having sex, as well as insisting he use a condom. Cathy took every precaution, because she had no desire to become a teenage mom.

Her safety measures failed her.

Her first Pap test several months later, prompted by her earlier request for birth control, did not go as she expected. Her doctor stopped the exam almost immediately, asking her to pee in a cup. While the doctor's wife held her hand, the doctor gently broke the news to her.

The very first time Cathy had sex is now a date she'll never forget. She's the warning story from the sex education video, where they say it only takes one time to get pregnant. Her initial reaction to the doctor's news was shock, and that feeling continued for years. Her situation didn't seem real.

"It's as if I was watching it happen to someone else."

Cathy walked home alone from her appointment and kept the secret for over two weeks. She went on with normal high school life and attended cadets as if nothing had changed, her mind secretly racing with worry over her future. Her dream of becoming a doctor through a career in the military was suddenly in jeopardy.

When she finally broke down and told her parents, their response lacked the comfort and reassurance she needed. Cathy's mother wept for days; her father took the news with booze. To make matters worse, they later gave her an ultimatum that thrust her further into adulthood than she was ready for at fifteen.

"I had the added pressure of having to figure out everything I was supposed to do on my own. I carried that as a tool to measure my success against what was expected of me. Whether what was expected of me was communicated or not, I had to know it all. I had to figure it out. Alone."

Cathy was already over five months along in her pregnancy, which limited her options. Her first instinct was to put the child up for adoption, but her parents vehemently rejected the idea. They wanted to raise the child as their own, and threatened to disown her if she gave the child to another family. Her own upbringing had been filled with constant criticism and poor parenting. She couldn't bear the thought of her child going through the same.

I need to describe Cathy to you as I know her now, before I explain the incredible steps she took to ensure both herself and her children would have the best life possible. She's a fighter. She has been knocked down throughout her life by the very people she should have been able to count on. Every time she falls, she rises stronger. And like most strong women, she doesn't give herself nearly enough credit for it.

> "I had a plan for my life from a young age. I knew the path I needed to take to create my dream life. I believe that the pregnancy became a gateway to an alternative life that came with strife and obstacles, which in turn brought out something in me that I didn't know was there."

Despite being a young teen, she had the drive and foresight to continue her education while pregnant, for as long as she could. Cathy stayed in school until they insisted that she leave, which was when she was seven months pregnant and it was too obvious to deny. She requested a tutor, who delivered and returned assignments on her behalf. She took her exams and passed everything with stellar grades. After following all of their instructions and putting in the work to pass with flying colors, the school tried to deny Cathy her diploma. She refused to back down, and eventually received the diploma she rightfully deserved.

> "Raising my son and myself at the same time was by far the biggest challenge I faced. Finishing school while being an independent teenage mom only made everything harder. The education system in the mid-nineties was not teen mom friendly. The available avenues through which one could obtain their high school diploma were limiting and difficult, almost shameful."

Shortly after giving birth, she rented an apartment on her own. Cathy was originally turned down for government-assisted childcare, but fought to ensure she had the financial means to continue her education. By age sixteen, Cathy was living a life that most young adults can't handle. She was a mom and a student, working a part-time job, and keeping up an apartment.

Where was the father?

Her relationship with her son's father ended before she found out she was pregnant. He didn't want her going away to cadet camp, and broke up with her over that decision. He didn't believe her when she first told him the news, and didn't tell his own parents until the day their son was born. The baby's father was several years older than Cathy, but he was far from ready for the same responsibilities she was about to manage on her own.

Cathy learned at a young age that the only person she could always rely on was herself. Her fierce determination and love for her children kept her going through year after year of ongoing struggles. When you're forced into adulthood before you have enough life experience to handle it, you're constantly playing catch up, financially and emotionally.

As someone who adores Cathy but also understands the impact of low self-esteem, I can see how her teenage years shaped her view of herself. Kids are cruel, and a pregnant fifteen-year-old is an easy target for derogatory remarks that make you question your worth. She was called a slut, a whore, and told she would never amount to anything. Those are harsh titles to shake.

Cathy now writes a passionate, personal blog about her experiences as a teen mom, *Raising the Woman Within*. She wants to show other teen moms that they are not defined by their past. In one of her blogs, she relates how her baby's father reacted in emotional detail.

"The moment was never going to be right, but he needed to know. He, being the father, the first man I had been with, the only man I had been with. Just like the moment when I told my parents the news, I sat there on the couch, frightened, shaking. I picked up the phone and dialed his number. Not prepared, not rehearsed, I asked for him. He came to the phone with what seemed to be an excited tone, one that proclaimed he was cool, calm, and charming as always. Too little too late, my voice cracked and the news spills out. 'I am pregnant, and it's yours.' Silence.

"The longest, most tense silence I have ever felt passed through the phone. His voice replied, 'Are you sure?' I said yes, still shaking. I can say from certainty in that moment I held my breath. I didn't want to make him mad. I didn't want to do this to him. He had a right to know. He had a right to an opinion. He had a right to a decision.

"Instead he said, in a blustering voice, 'It's not mine, can't be. I know you slept with other guys; your friends told me. So, it can't be mine.' I assured him that he was the father. He still didn't believe me. 'No, it's not. You're a slut, a whore, everyone knows it.' He hung up. He was angry, he was in disbelief, just as much as I, myself, still was. I was hurt and alone.

"How could he say those things? I gave him a piece of me that no one else will ever have. How could he think of me that way? He was my first, my only. How could he throw that moment away like it was nothing? What in the world was he talking about?! I was baffled. I ran up to my room, cried the remainder of the night through until morning."

She was shamed for doing the exact same thing he did. Twenty-five years later, she still battles those feelings and has to remind herself that she's worthy of a good life. This is a brave young girl who worked her ass off to care for her children, to secure her education and a solid career. Her life has been an uphill journey and she continues to rise. She has every reason to feel proud, but the opinions and demands of others dragged her down to rock bottom.

"I am really not sure if there was ever one poignant moment that made me want to give up. It was more an accumulation of moments. Slowly, I gave up trying to discover my passion, I gave up on being a woman. I gave up on thinking that I deserved that job, that car, that pair of shoes. I had simply given up without realizing it.

"From having my son at fifteen, I gave up on my dream to work as a trauma physician in the military. My marriage broke down after being cheated on by my husband and financial distress. I was being pulled every which way, by everyone around me. I had nothing for myself. I let myself deteriorate without noticing, always knowing deep down that I was not enough; so what was the point?"

Fortunately, she's a survivor and didn't let those self-deprecating thoughts or the behavior of others slow her climb. Cathy knows deep down that she was and is a great mother. She's a solo homeowner with an impressive job at the local hospital, and she's loved by many friends.

"Raising my normal-*ish* children is my greatest accomplishment. Hearing my son say, 'Mom, I know that I didn't have the greatest childhood, but it wasn't that bad. You did good, Mom." Proud mom moment there! Definitely obtaining my high school and college degrees. Overcoming the stigma of being a teen mom. Making it on my own after a toxic marriage. Starting over."

Life is filled with tough moments that we think will break us. Cathy didn't allow an unexpected, yet permanent aspect of her younger years affect her future potential. She used it as a catalyst to break free from a toxic home life and build a solid foundation for her own family. When something didn't work out, she simply found another way that did.

Although the specific details are quite different, the next woman ready to rise has conquered similar challenges. I've known Deb for twenty years, and she never ceases to amaze me. Her life has been filled with tough obstacles, but you could have a hundred conversations with her and never know she's experienced any hardships.

Deb doesn't dwell on the tough times from her past, or the setbacks that still occur throughout her life. Her optimistic outlook and generous nature give the impression that she's walking on easy street. In reality, the hardships she has overcome are why she's extraordinarily appreciative of every blessing in her life. In her own words:

"I have faced a number of challenges throughout the course of my life, but no matter how impossible they may have seemed to overcome while I was going through them, I always came out smiling—and stronger. I am a fighter, and I am a true believer that whatever doesn't kill you makes you stronger, and that absolutely everything happens for a reason. There is so much opportunity to learn from everything you go through, good and bad, which will always make you wiser, stronger, and more compassionate."

She has that optimistic perspective, even though Deb spent the first thirteen years of her life in an unstable, toxic environment that left her with childhood memories of criminal activity and neglect.

"I was born into a very broken and dysfunctional family. I was the youngest of four children (the first three were from my mom's previous marriage). I was raised by a single mom, and my dad didn't have a whole lot to do with me. Both my parents were alcoholics, and my siblings were drug users. I was witness to abuse, neglect, and crime; this was my 'normal.'

"As a young girl approaching high school, my aspiration was to sell drugs for my oldest brother. I was headed in a bad direction. Then one of the most tragic things happened, but out of this tragedy came a tremendous opportunity—and *it happened for a reason*. My mom got sick: lung cancer. I was only thirteen."

Deb's mom passed away shortly after, and her entire world was twisted upside down. The pain of losing a parent at such a turbulent age hurts, regardless of the parent's behavior. It took time, but Deb found the blessing in disguise. She was eagerly adopted by a wonderful young couple who helped redirect her life onto a more productive path. Deb's new family was a stark contrast to the only life she had ever known; like most transitions, there were a few bumps along the way.

"They were amazing people with strong morals and values, and they worked hard for a living. They taught me generosity, kindness, support, and honesty. They showed me life could be different.

"It was not easy, by any means: I had, after all, been ripped from the only life I had ever known and thrown into a brand new one, full of strangers and their ridiculous rules. It took some time, but we all adjusted well. I was on my way to becoming a better person."

Deb made mistakes along the way, but the experience fueled her with the empathy and gratitude she shows others today. Rising from being raised in a dysfunctional family is a story worth telling, however, that's only a part of why I knew she had to be in this story. Like Cathy, Deb was a teenage mom.

I've been a part of Deb's life since the kids were quite young, and she's an extraordinary mom. She's the kind of mom I'd be if I had total say (stepmoms have closer to zero say), and I believe her motherly skills are a direct reflection of her "chosen" mother, Kathy.

Kathy is not one of the women I interviewed, but I need to pause for a moment to send some kudos in her direction. She was fairly young when she made the decision to adopt Deb, because she was an adoptee whose "chosen" mother changed her life. Kathy was inspired to do the same for Deb, when she saw her world falling apart as she was entering into her teenage years.

"I have always been driven, but getting the support and guidance from my new family, my new mom, made all the difference in the world. I knew I needed to rise up so that I could be a better person (better than where I came from) and to show my mom I was grateful for everything she has done for me. Then I had to rise up so that I could teach my children that life is what you make of it and that they too, can overcome anything."

Kathy's mix of compassion and tough love gave Deb the confidence she needed to feel joy when she discovered she was pregnant at eighteen. Most teenagers' first reaction would be fear, panic, or total devastation, but not Deb's. I asked her if she had ever considered ending the pregnancy, or adoption, and her response is as charming and forthright as I'd expect from my lifelong friend.

"No, I never considered it. When I found out I was pregnant, I was nervous, but too young and dumb to be scared. I was 99% excited. I knew I was going to be a mom."

Deb is a fantastic mom. However, her parenting experiences have been less than ideal. Creating the child was obviously a two-person endeavor, so she assumed raising the child would be as well. Whereas Deb found the courage and commitment to rise to the responsibility of becoming a young mom, the male half of the equation lacked the same sense of duty.

"I rushed into things way too quickly with a young man—let's call him Jack—and it turned out we weren't a good fit. This realization came too late, since we were expecting my first child. We were already a couple longer than we should have been, but everything happens for a reason. The decision to leave him came when I realized that I was becoming miserable. I was feeling angry all the time. This was not me.

"I pondered the decision to leave him while I sat holding my beautiful little baby girl, and it quickly became clear that staying with him wasn't even an option. I could either stay with him and be miserable, which was no example to set for my perfect little daughter, or my happy, positive self could raise her on my own. Done deal. Single it was."

Once "Jack" realized that a romantic relationship with Deb was not a part of the parenting deal, his involvement decreased drastically. Coincidentally, their roles as parents increased *dramatically*. Doubled, in fact, two days before her daughter's first birthday.

"Shortly after I left Jack, I learned that I was expecting again—and I was already four months along! Yikes! Raising my little girl on my own was already a challenge, and funds were extremely tight, bordering on impossible. How on earth would I manage doing this with two babies?

"I would manage because I didn't know I couldn't, that's how. Now I was a single mother of two, working part-time for minimum wage, in college, and exhausted. Kids, work, and school were my life—in that order.

"Jack wasn't very helpful with the babies, so I fought for child support in hopes he could at least contribute financially. Since Jack was an entertainer and mostly paid in cash, which he would boast about freely, the courts awarded me a total of $200 per month—only $100 per kid. That's OK, though. I would manage. I always did. I ended up having to withdraw from my college program before I finished because I needed to work full time to support my family."

I've known Deb a long time, and I can hear her defiant optimism in every answer. It doesn't matter how turbulent life gets; she rises to every occasion. She wasn't willing to stay with someone who didn't make her happy, and she couldn't force her ex to pay his fair share. That left her only one option: figure out a way to handle everything on her own. So that is what she did, to the best of her abilities, for the next few years.

"The last thing I wanted was the complication of another relationship on top of everything else I had on my plate, so I avoided boys for several years. Eventually I met and developed a friendship with a man who seemed like a good guy. We'll call him Richard.

"The friendship turned into more, and I found myself pregnant again. I was overcome by uncertainty and doubt at the thought of a third child. It was with a man who seemed nice, but I was still scared.

"I worked up the courage to tell Richard about the brand-new life growing inside me. He seemed so happy to learn we were expecting. I couldn't believe my ears! After talking with him, I was on top of the world, thinking everything was going to be just fine! And it was, and it is. It always is fine. It just didn't turn out the way I was hoping it would.

"Richard stopped coming by and wasn't returning my phone calls. I wasn't sure what was going on, so I stopped in to see him. That was when I learned that he was not planning on being a part of the baby's life after all. He had other plans with other women, unbeknownst to me, and 'having a baby would ruin everything' for him. Fine. I'd been a single mother of two for several years, and I was managing it. What's one more kid?

"My third baby was born in November 2002, and still to this day, Richard has not been part of his life: not physically, emotionally, or financially. I fought for child support because this is the very least he could do, but he quits his job each time his employment is reported. It's his loss, and it's tragic. This kid is amazing!"

Three small children, $200 in child support, and dreams of going back to school to finish her education. A seemingly impossible scenario for most people, but not Deb. Life continued to throw up hurdles—like her youngest having asthma when she didn't have any medical coverage—but she always found a way to make it over each obstacle and kept moving forward.

"I would have to say that my whole life as a mother has been my biggest accomplishment. I have always loved them more than life itself, spent 97% of every minute trying to set a good example for them. (I lost all rational thought and flew off the handle the other 3%.) I've worked very hard to support myself and my kids.

"Understanding the value of an education and knowing I wanted to provide a good, financially stable life for my family, I went back to school in 2005 and finished my advertising and marketing program in 2008. My diploma allowed me to start a more lucrative career that I love passionately."

Everything happens for a reason, and everything eventually works itself out. Deb lives by both of those philosophies and they've helped her through losing her parents, teenage pregnancy, failed relationships, and financial struggles.

"There are definitely circumstances that made me feel defeated and had me wanting to give up, but these feelings were short lived, even though some of the circumstances weren't."

Despite her best efforts not to fall in love again, Deb did end up meeting the love of her life a couple years after her third child was born. They married in 2007, and are still quite smitten with each other. Her babies are now entering adulthood. She has a stable, well-paying career, a loving husband, and the same unbreakable strength she's carried with her since childhood. No matter what happens in her future, Deb is a woman ready to rise.

Deb and Cathy are both teenage mom success stories. My mom is as well, and since I started writing this book, I've met several other women whose unintentional pregnancies blossomed into intention fulfilling, strength-building, tales of triumph. Although I may currently be known as an author who speaks up for the childfree choice in *No Kids Required*, I have genuine respect for moms.

For many women, pregnancy awakens this loving, giving being who is ready to sacrifice everything for the person growing inside of them. That definitely was how those teen moms felt, but this brand of selfless parenting can be seen in all sorts of situations.

I have a friend Sarah who chose to have her son fully aware that his father (or accidental sperm donor) would never be in the picture, and her own family lived too far away to offer any substantial support. She knew it wouldn't be easy to raise a child completely on her own, because child-rearing truly takes a village. Knowing it would be harder than it should didn't stop Sarah from having the chance to raise her child.

Sarah was certain that she was meant to be a mom, and figured out ways to make it work. She is raising a fine young gentleman, has a pretty impressive job, and can proudly claim that she did it completely on her own. Now, she's met a loving man and is voluntarily helping to raise his three girls and her son in a hectic, accepting home.

With the same determination, I know fierce women who are willing to fight for the chance to be a mom, regardless of the methods it might take. My friend Stacey struggled with infertility for years. Her desire to become a mother was so strong that she put her body through several rounds of IVF and other expensive fertility treatments. You'll have to wait until I share her full story, near the end of the book, to see how everything worked out for Stacey.

My Aunt Liz is one of the most generous and loving souls I know, yet she didn't fall in love until quite a bit later in life. She wasn't able to give all that love she had inside to a biological child once she was finally ready to try, but that didn't stop her pursuit of becoming a mom. In her early forties, she and my uncle began the adoption process and ended up with not one, but two absolute blessings. My cousins were adopted a year apart, one at 20 months and the other at two-and-half years old.

It's beautiful to see these two kids thrive when they would have possibly faced a life full of hardships and challenges, maybe even worse than Katelynn's experience in foster care. My aunt and uncle have the resources and genuine compassion to accept both as their own and give them every opportunity that they may not have had otherwise.

Mothers who do their best to raise good children are the very definition of women ready to rise. They pour their hearts and time into lifting and assisting children who will share our future. Whether you're a teen mom, single mom, foster mom, adopted mom, stepmom, or any other form of raising the next generation, you are a woman ready to rise.

THE NEVER EMPTY NEST

Katelynn found the strength to overcome the loss of her child; Cathy and Deb were capable of successfully raising children while still practically being children themselves. What about having to tackle essentially both of these challenges at once? Losing the child whom you had expected to raise, yet still having to raise a child whose demands far exceed your current capabilities (or so it feels).

That highly-emotional and complex reality describes what one of my longtime friends experienced. Kimberly was the second name that came to mind when I decided to write this story, and immediately earned an entire chapter. Every aspect of Kimberly's life has been jam-packed with the knock-the-wind-out-of-you kind of obstacles, yet she keeps getting back up and fighting.

As teenagers, we were very similar. We both excelled in school. However, we did get into our share of trouble. We bonded over bad habits and learned many lessons along the way. Although she is extraordinary, she was and is just as ordinary as the rest of us. No one, including her, knew she had the strength to handle the greatest heartache a parent can face until she was forced to do so.

Kimberly's second child has cerebral palsy. He is severely disabled, and will require full-time care for his entire life. She was already a heavily-involved stepmom to one son and a busy mom to her young daughter, but the thought of raising a quadriplegic child was incredibly overwhelming.

After Kimberly submitted her answers to my questions for this book, she followed it up with this flashback to the moment her life changed forever. I would like to share how that singular moment impacted her world, using her own words.

"I was just thinking today about when Liam was born and in the NICU. I remember thinking, *Why me? Why him? How is this fair?*

"I was sitting outside the hospital and overheard a conversation between a new mother and her friend. She was bragging about how healthy her new baby was, despite having smoked during her pregnancy. Needless to say, this really upset me. I did everything right during my pregnancy: ate right, took the supplements, attended all my prenatal appointments, didn't smoke, didn't drink... But my baby Liam is fighting for his life. And here's a woman who was reckless and careless during her pregnancy, and has a perfectly healthy baby.

"Why would God do this to me? Why punish me and bless her?

"But I see it differently now. I see now that I was blessed with being Liam's mom. I feel that God chose me to be his mom because he knew I would rise to the challenge of selflessly taking care of him and giving him the best life possible."

I know Kimberly quite well, and can confirm she has done just that. She has far exceeded the expectations of the average mom, and given her son more hope than anyone thought possible. She rose to the challenge, and keeps rising above every roadblock that tries to stop her.

Kimberly is a woman determined to rise.

I personally didn't know that much about the demands and monstrous obstacles that would accompany such a diagnosis until I interviewed Kimberly in person. I've Googled the terms *cerebral palsy* and *severe quadriplegic* numerous times since Kimberly gave birth to Liam, but its impact has never quite sunk in. I watch his slow, yet remarkably impressive progress and try to grasp the work it must take. Admittedly, I was quite clueless until I had the privilege to delve into her kickass story.

Unless you are in this situation, you can't quite comprehend the commitment it takes. I'm devoting this entire chapter to explaining all of the steps Kimberly has taken to give her son—and of course her daughter and stepson, as well—the absolute best life possible. For her older children, she will guide them into adulthood and be a fixture watching from the sidelines, as parents should do once their kids are grown. That won't be how it works with Liam.

I messaged Kimberly when I came up with the title for this chapter, because "The Never Empty Nest" sounds like I don't have faith he'll ever become independent. I know she believes anything is possible for Liam, and works her ass off to ensure every miracle is fulfilled. Reality is much harsher.

> "Is it insensitive to assume you'll always have him home? I know he's making great strides. Is that title accurate, or insulting?" I asked.
> "That title is perfect," Kimberly responded.

She is fully aware that the commitment she has made goes far beyond her decision to become a parent. Although he's making leaps and bounds due to Kimberly's pursuit of the best for her son, there's still very little chance of him ever being able to care for himself or live on his own. While most moms are waiting for some much-needed relief when their teens finally transition into their twenties, she knows that Liam will need her constant care for the entirety of his life.

Like every parent, she hopes his life will exceed her own. That addresses a serious concern that she hasn't quite resolved: Who will care for Liam when she's gone? Her daughter loves and helps take care of her little brother now, but who knows if she'll have the resources or time to give him the daily assistance that he needs? How can she ask anyone to take over such life-changing responsibilities? I thank my lucky stars not to be in Kimberly's shoes.

Yet Kimberly doesn't see it that way. She believes she was given Liam because she is strong enough to raise him right and that he is a blessing, not a burden on her life. That perspective inspired her to push harder, asking more from herself than what's expected from a mother of a severely disabled child.

"Liam is my greatest accomplishment. At two years old, the doctors and therapists said that, based on his skill level at that time, he would never sit unassisted, never walk, never talk, and would need to be buckled in a chair for the rest of his life. My response was 'challenge accepted,' LOL.

"Liam wasn't being seen as an individual. He was being seen as a child with cerebral palsy who had only acquired a certain skill set by two years old, which indicated to the doctors what his future would be based on other kids 'like him.' Well, I found this unfair and thought to myself, *you don't know me, and you don't know my son. I will not give up on him or place limits on him. I will do everything I can to give him every opportunity at a better quality of life.*"

This fierce woman is a fighter. Prior to being tossed into the life of an advocate for children with cerebral palsy, Kimberly was a customs officer at our Canadian/US Border. She had to relocate for months and went through extensive training. Despite her small physical stature, "Lil' Kim" had what it takes to defend our country. Fear was not a factor when it came to raising Liam.

On the cerebral palsy scale, Liam is a four out of five for severity, meaning his brain does not communicate with his muscles. Everything we are born knowing how to do, Liam had to learn. It took days before he was able to cry. The doctor was hesitant to turn him on his back because he didn't have the natural instinct to swallow.

Thankfully, his mom wanted more for and from him than their limited expectations, right from day one. When the doctor suggested giving Liam medication to reduce the saliva so that they could attempt to put him on his back, Kimberly had a better idea.

36

"Can we try putting him on his back without it, and see if he swallows on his own? If he's unable to do it, *then* we can try the medication."

The doctor agreed, and Kimberly's instincts were right. He never needed it. This was the first step in pushing for a better life for Liam, and the successful first time she spoke up, gave her the confidence to keep testing his limits.

The doctors and therapists would say, "We'll wait and see what he can do."

Kimberly would respond, "Let's try pushing him to do more, so we can see what he can really do."

Liam was supposed to require a feeding tube; that's the expectation for his CP level of severity, and the standard solution given by doctors. Kimberly wasn't willing to accept his limitations based on the abilities of a typical quadriplegic; she first wanted to see what Liam was capable of doing on his own. She insisted on trying to feed him without it, and guess what? He's never needed one.

Although she continued to triumph over every challenge, this has been her life for the past ten years. Every day is a battle, and nothing comes easy. From the moment in the hospital when she realized her life would never be the same again, Kimberly has had to wake up each day ready to fight for her son.

You may be wondering at this point where Liam's father is during all of these tough moments. Kimberly was married to him, raising their sweet daughter and her stepson, living a relatively content life prior to Liam's birth. Although it didn't happen instantly, the strain of the situation rattled the once happy home.

Her ex was incapable of being the father Liam needed. Over time, the marriage broke apart. Following the divorce, he ceased being a part of both her daughter's and Liam's life. That only gave Kimberly more reasons to do everything she could to give her children the best possible future.

"Liam's disability led me to give up on my career and my marriage, but for positive, good reasons. I was in an unhealthy marriage, and I wanted my children to be raised in the best environment possible. Liam's disability and dependence on me gave me the strength to know that I could do it. I tried to balance my career while caring for Liam's needs, but ultimately it became apparent that he needed me more. In order to help him improve, I needed to be home full time. So, I devoted my time to being the best mom I could."

Kimberly has fallen in love again, with a great guy who treats her kids as his own. But she's still the primary caregiver for Liam, and she will be for as long as she is alive and able. She gave up her job and financial security for the only priority that actually mattered.

Although she's achieved some amazing feats on her own, Kimberly realized early on that she would need as much help as she could recruit to give him every advantage that was available. Of course, Liam's maternal grandparents and paternal grandmother were eager to do whatever they could, as were other close family and friends.

Those who love her and the kids would always do what they could to make it easier for their family. However, Kimberly wasn't interested in pursuing the easy way out. She wanted the absolute best for her son, and didn't let the price tag stop her from trying.

After relentless searching for better options than the standard one hour a week of therapy Liam was offered, she found a conductive education therapy program in Toronto that would give him the intense therapy that he needed. The only problem was that it would cost over $10,000 for the four-week program, including her stay in Toronto.

The program was six weeks away, and no one in her family had anywhere near that amount simply sitting in a bank. That's when Kimberly turned into a fundraising queen. With the help of family and friends, she hosted a big event, gathered prizes to raffle away, and raised more than she needed. For five years, she repeated these efforts, as well as partaking in a large yard sale, so he could continue expanding on his muscle development, temperament, and motor skills.

Each time he attends the therapy, Liam comes out with new capabilities. In the beginning, it was tiny steps, like making eye contact and relaxing his hands, which had always been tightly fisted. Then his progress increased into sitting up and rolling over. The combination of Kimberly encouraging him to try things doctors didn't think were possible and the extra cognitive therapy Liam has received built solid connections between his brain and his muscles that never existed before. He is not only doing things he wasn't expected to do, he is remembering and repeating the tasks.

Here's a little glimpse into the extra obstacles Kimberly hurdles without thinking. Liam had frightening seizures several times, before he was put on the proper medication to prevent it. One of these occurred when she was staying in Toronto (400 miles away from home), which resulted in her and Liam being rushed to the hospital in an ambulance. Thankfully, he was fine.

This meant Kimberly and Liam were stuck at the hospital, without a car seat to take him back to their hotel. It was very late in the evening and had been an obviously stressful day, so she had to find a hotel for the night. In the morning, she was lucky enough to find a compassionate cab driver who was willing to drive her back to the apartment she had rented for a month, even though Liam was not in a car seat.

Kimberly was cool as a cucumber throughout. Even the ambulance attendant commented on how calm she was in a situation that would have most mothers shaking in tears. I'm certain she was terrified on the inside, but staying strong and powering through extreme crisis was a technique Kimberly had mastered by that point in Liam's life.

She's developed quite a few new skills since Liam was born—fundraising being one of the most essential, yet not the most impressive. She has immersed herself in studying new ways to bring out the best in Liam. If there is an opportunity to help her children, she pursues it diligently and with purpose.

In 2016, after a big growth spurt, Liam's legs were becoming very tight. His bones were growing at a rate so great that his muscles and tendons couldn't keep up. He was beginning to lose the ability to stand and bear any weight, which would prevent him from ever walking. He couldn't stand flat on his feet when his feet were stuck in a pointed position.

"One of my contacts from the therapy sessions told me about a non-invasive outpatient surgery done in New York called selective percutaneous myofascial lengthening, or SPML. After hundreds of hours of research and networking with parents who had the procedure done for their children, I decided I needed to do what was necessary to get this surgery for Liam. I wanted to give him the ability to continue expanding on his functional skills and reach his full potential."

The thought of giving him a chance at walking not only inspired Kimberly, it gave hope to everyone who loved him, as well as strangers who were touched by his story. With the help of friends and family, another fundraiser was planned. Kimberly also launched a GoFundMe account for the surgery. A year of promoting and praying resulted in raising the funds to pay for the $18,000 procedure.

In the summer of 2017, Kimberly, her mom, her daughter, and Liam traveled to New York for the big day. It was a quick outpatient surgery, allowing them to incorporate a small vacation and tour of New York into their visit. Family vacations were something that occurred less frequently after Liam's birth.

Following the surgery, Liam went through another five-week intensive therapy session, allowing him to start using his legs and arms again. During his therapeutic horseback riding, Liam went from needing full core support to sitting up tall and independently while riding the horse. This was attributed to the relaxed nature of his legs post surgery.

Kimberly has continued with the intensive therapy sessions annually, and Liam is now working on walking independently using a walker. Every step he takes is a huge leap forward for her family. Kimberly pushes her own limits to ensure he doesn't have any, and she celebrates every blessing that comes from her difficult situation. That's what makes Kimberly a woman ready to rise.

"I have met families from all over North America and developed great friendships along the way, all as a result of attending these therapy sessions. I learned how to assist Liam with whatever he needs, and to continue the daily therapy sessions at home.

"After seeing the benefits of the therapy sessions out of town, I felt that all children deserve the opportunity to reach their full potential. Unfortunately, I knew that it was financially out of reach for most families. I was determined to find a way to make it available to other children locally, at a cost that was affordable.

"I discovered a program located in Chatham, as well as two other locations in southern Ontario, with a cost to families of only $200. This was made possible through year-long fundraising efforts by the Southwestern Optimist Clubs.

"Liam and I attend their summer camp in Chatham, so I asked the director about adding a summer camp in Windsor. He said that as long as I could get enough families, they would love to expand. I went to work, informing local families of the opportunity and recruiting those interested in the program. The following summer, we had the first camp in Windsor. I work hard every year to keep it going, because I know the positive impact it has on kids like Liam."

Kimberly is only one woman, but the ripple effect of her efforts has impacted so many other parents who are desperate to create some normalcy and sense of accomplishment for their disabled children. From major changes like inspiring the summer camp to smaller success stories like convincing our city to install a really cool swing for disabled kids at a local park, Kimberly strives to improve the lives of our most vulnerable children.

The lengths Kimberly has gone to, determined to ensure Liam has every opportunity, benefits more than just other families with similar struggles. Kimberly manages a Facebook page, *No Limits for Liam*, that I highly recommend everyone follows. Watching him thrive and live up to his true potential inspires hope in everyone. If Liam can push himself to surpass all expectations, so can you!

I took a peek at the page while I was wrapping up the chapter, and discovered Liam has a new milestone. His dietician has always calculated his caloric requirements and prescribed the necessary high-calorie nutritional supplements to maintain the right weight for Liam's age and size.

"Well, after 10 years, Liam is no longer drinking the special nutritional drinks because he is eating the same amount of food as other kids his age!!! He just woke up one morning and decided he wanted to eat a ton. For example, this morning he ate four Eggo pancakes for breakfast!! Never give up, never impose limits, be patient, stay determined, keep the faith, follow your intuition, and celebrate every milestone, no matter how big or small."

At the beginning of this chapter, Kimberly expressed how she felt when Liam was first born: *Why me? Why my son?* Her instinctive, gut reaction was natural and understandable. She knew her life would be changed forever, but she didn't realize it would be this incredible blessing.

"If Liam had been born as a 'typical' child, I would have had a typical life: working full time, doing typical mom things. I would have never learned how to appreciate the simple things in life. I now look at children in awe of each milestone they reach because I understand the complexity of the things that we all take for granted. Things as simple as holding a toy."

As her daughter becomes a teen in an increasingly complicated society and Liam learns new tricks, Kimberly's parenting abilities are constantly being challenged. After everything she's been through, there's nothing her kids could say or do that she wouldn't find a way through with gratitude.

As tough as Kimberly's life is to manage, she knows that it could always be worse. Writing about her story reminded me of how blessed I truly am;

I hope it shows you that there is no circumstance so impossible that you can't find hope for a better future. It may be a never-empty nest for Kimberly, but that's because the nest is overflowing with love.

AWAKENINGS &
SECOND CHANCES

I wrote the introduction to the next warrior woman's story in my head, while driving home from a women's event where she was the guest speaker. I've heard Tina tell her story at several events prior to that particular one, but this was the most vulnerable she had been. It was the first time I saw myself reflected in her confessions. Tina had a less than perfect childhood that led to many poor choices as a young adult, and now she's finally learned how to love herself.

Tina grew up in an unstable home with parents who were struggling to take proper care of themselves, let alone her. When her mother left and her father sank into a toxic depression, Tina held herself responsible. She thought if she could only be perfect, her home life would suddenly be perfect too.

"I spent many years pretending to be someone who I wasn't. I thought that if I looked perfect on the outside, people would not see how broken I was on the inside. I thought I was broken because I was raised in an unpredictable environment. My parents were big drinkers and after their divorce, my dad became very mentally ill.

"He struggled with depression, anxiety...and mixing booze with that was not a good combo for him. He developed really bad habits, which ultimately led him to many psychiatric ward visits and multiple suicide attempts. I never wanted to be the person that people felt sorry for, so I hid a lot of emotions and truth about what was going on in my head and life."

No matter what she was going through or how those in her life treated her, Tina held herself to a higher standard. She was determined to have an impressive career, a happy marriage, and a perfect home life. She was going to give herself everything that was missing from her upbringing.

Tina went to university to become a teacher, excelling in social service work and classroom positions. She soon had the lucrative career she always imagined. She met a great guy, had two adorable children, and everything looked the way she envisioned on the outside.

Tina created an illusion of perfection, while beating herself up in her mind for not being able to actually achieve it. Her love for education quickly soured, with the reality of the rigid curriculum and classroom format. She found herself longing for the end of the day, the next holiday, or summer vacation. Tina was drained and uninspired. The lack of passion for her day job rolled over into her marriage, and she felt the need to leave her husband after sixteen years.

To rebel from the structure of the classroom and a life of trying to be perfect, Tina started celebrating her new-found freedom by partying like she did when she was a teenager. She amped up her life of the party status into a reckless rebellion of potentially-permanent mistakes. Her self-control slowly slipped away.

I find this part of her story incredibly relatable. My mom went through a similar, somewhat destructive phase in her late twenties; so did I, in my mid-thirties. I have several friends who were really responsible from their late teens to early twenties, then went hog wild in their thirties. I think women need to completely let go from time to time and enjoy some reckless fun. When we lose ourselves in an experience, we often end up finding a part of ourselves we never knew existed.

Unfortunately, in Tina's case, the drinking became excessive and destructive. She recalls a time when she was too drunk to drive, but did it anyway. In the talk I just heard from her, she admitted to driving with a friend and his kids in the car, but not being able to remember it the next morning. Please don't judge her; I know I've made similar potentially-deadly mistakes.

We're all just fucking human.

"After my separation from my husband of 12 years, I developed an addiction to alcohol. I spent many nights drunk and often wondered how I made it home. My almost rock bottom happened after a Christmas party. I was so drunk I didn't remember driving home; I got up in the morning and was *still* too drunk to drive.

"I went to my nurse practitioner and told her I couldn't cope with life. I was anxious, I couldn't sleep, I was depressed... I didn't tell her I was also drunk every day. She prescribed me antidepressants and sleeping pills."

She had her wake-up call and was determined to put her life back together, but pills weren't the solution for her. Tina decided to quit drinking and become truly healthy, physically and mentally. She enrolled in a program to become a health coach, discovered her love of helping other people, and has even quit her six-figure teaching salary and pension to pursue her health coaching business permanently.

"I had to own my shit and take responsibility for the way I was living my life. Once I realized that I created my stories and I can change them, my world opened up. It wasn't my dad's fault, or my mom's, or my husband's, or my relationship, but *me*! I was the common denominator...then I knew that I was going to be my savior. I was going to pull myself out. That was the first step."

Tina's still an overachiever, but she does it now because she's passionate about her life purpose. A few years ago, she recognized how the stories she told herself throughout her childhood were still affecting her life today. She was still fighting this fear that she'd grow up to be like her parents, or feel compelled to chase impossible perfection while living in a delusion with no satisfaction.

Once Tina was able to rationalize and separate the story she had created in her head from the reality of her life, she realized her imperfections had no bearing on her parents' broken lives. She was able to forgive her parents, celebrate herself and her achievements, and pass along this powerful lesson to others.

> "I am a person who is positive and capable of choosing to live life on my terms. I'm a great role model, and only want to help bring out the best in others. I am ready to put my childhood stories to bed and create the life I want to live."

Her confidence doesn't come from thinking she's superior; she now accepts herself fully and knows she's in control of her actions and attitude. Tina has flaws, because like all of us, she was born to flawed parents who were the product of flawed parenting. Perfect parenting doesn't exist, because perfect people are an impossibility.

When she was beating herself up for her imperfections, she couldn't find peace with herself. She couldn't be happy. It didn't matter how many outstanding reasons Tina had to be proud of herself, she would never feel good enough until she could accept that failing to be perfect is not failing.

Now, Tina gets it.

Realizing that the pressures and expectations were preventing her from truly being happy changed everything. She dug deep and found what she really wanted to do with her life, and it transitioned from being about the things she needed to achieve into creating a life that gave her the feelings she deserved to feel.

Tina's focus shifted to strengthening her relationship with her kids by being honest, transparent, and inquisitive. She uses the same self-awareness type of questions that she used to find her purpose to get down to the root of how her daughters feel. When I asked Tina to list her greatest accomplishments, her daughters topped the list.

"Number one: raising my daughters to be amazing human beings. They are kind, loving, thoughtful, and smart. They are my light on dark days."

Her new, clearer perspective in life is seen in her daughter's beaming smiles. Tina understands the pressure, expectations, and negative self-talk that lead to low self-esteem in so many women. She will ensure her daughters don't tell themselves the same self-destructive stories that she used to tell herself.

Tina realized she was also creating stories about her marriage that contributed to its sudden failure. Her husband was a good man, a devoted father, and their love existed at one time. Once she was honest with herself, Tina was able to be open with him and they are now happily reunited after three years apart. The truth is that the stable home Tina deserved was always within her reach; she only needed convincing that she was worthy of it.

Shortly after I first met Tina, she was selected to be a TEDx Windsor speaker. It was something I had applied for as well, twice, without success. We were connecting over dinner with two other like-minded women, and she confessed that she felt unworthy of the honor. This was a few years ago, when she was just starting to rebuild her confidence after taking control of her life again. Doubts and insecurities were still nagging at her self-esteem.

Instead of telling herself that she wasn't good enough to apply, she submitted an enthusiastic and enlightening video showcasing why she deserved to be a speaker. She ignored the insecure story in her head of not being worthy and created her own story, in which she was the most confident and credible woman for TEDx.

I was lucky enough to volunteer the day Tina shared her revelation and heard her eloquently express how we can create the life we want by shaping the stories we tell ourselves. Now Tina is sharing her wisdom with others as a coach and mentor. She knows and owns her own missteps, and is guiding others down better paths.

"I was inspired by my clients who were putting in the work and achieving amazing results. I was inspired by my children, whom I saw blossom in front of my eyes. Their voices were becoming echoes of my voice, and I knew I was making an impact. The faith I had in myself and my unwavering belief that I will make a difference pushed me when I wanted to quit. I knew in my soul that I am destined to make a difference, and I will."

Tina understands that the power is in her hands, and she is now writing the story she wants to live. Her mental fortitude gave her the strength she needed to rise before she had sunk too low, and now she's lifting others so they won't drown in negative thoughts. Her life may not have been easy, and she's far from perfect, but Tina is worthy of the best life possible—just like you!

My next lovely lady is Lisa, and this is not the first time I've shared a portion of Lisa's life in one of my books. I briefly touched on her experiences in *Dark Confessions of an Extraordinary, Ordinary Woman*, when I discovered how similar our past relationships had been. Both of us put up with shit that we shouldn't have, and turned our toughest moments into our greatest strengths.

This was a private message Lisa sent me six years ago, and it's kismet that I'm now writing her own personal story:

"I'm intrigued by people and what their lives have entailed. We hide behind our own walls until we meet someone who has been through difficulty. When I read your book title, I had no idea you wrote about your own personal journey. I remember thinking to myself, *does she know about my life?*"

It's crazy how intricately our lives are entwined with countless others. When we pull back those walls, we can find similarities in how we handle the hardest moments. Human beings crave connection, and lifting someone else up when they've fallen creates a lasting bond.

There was another reference to Lisa in my first book, and it's the reason we're forever intertwined. She gave me that helping hand the first time a boy physically assaulted me. After an ex-boyfriend punched me in the face repeatedly, Lisa walked me home to make sure I made it there safely. We were so young, but I'll always remember how kind she was to someone she barely knew at the time.

I met Lisa when she was on the cusp of becoming a teenager and watched her blossom with every life experience. She was noticeably over-weight in grade school, as a problem with her kidneys was causing her to retain water. She was over 200 pounds as a young teenager and had to deal with ignorant insults from arrogant jocks. Their remarks and a successful kidney surgery resulted in Lisa slowly losing over 100 pounds prior to her final year of high school.

> "Their insults motivated me. I was determined to prove them wrong."

Lisa fell in love shortly after finishing school, and caved in to pres-sure to get married when she was only 24 years old. He was her best friend's cousin, and they hung out all the time. Their union seemed destined, in the beginning. In time, both of them realized they were set-tling out of convenience. Their love felt more platonic and lacked any real passion. Her first attempt at happily-ever-after failed less than two years after saying, "I do."

Always resilient and hopeful, Lisa gave love another chance and met the second love of her life a few years later. He was a co-worker with two young kids. She felt the passion that had been missing in her mar-riage, and gained an overwhelming sense of compassion for his son and daughter. She warmly accepted her role as stepmother and cherished their family time together. What Lisa didn't know at the time was that her new love had a prior history of opioid addiction.

> "Being with Rich changed me. I became more loving and emotional. I let my guard down."

Lisa's second relationship went off in a dark direction after a trip to Mexico, where Rich was prescribed Percocet for a groin pull. Unaware of his past, she assumed things went back to normal once they returned from vacation. They were living together and deeply in love; it took time for her to realize that she was living with an addict.

"He was slurring, sweaty, and clammy. His daughter once told me a story about him frantically searching for something in the trash because it was so important. Now I wonder if it was drugs. I would find a random pill once in awhile, but I could never prove it was from him. He would take so many pills that he would vomit, and then he'd take some more. I knew he needed help."

Rich's addiction quickly became too serious for him to deny. Lisa finally called him out for his unacceptable attitude and uncontrollable mood swings when his behavior ruined her employer's Christmas party. The threat of losing everything he loved was enough for him to get clean.

A sober friend guided Rich into rehab, where he willingly committed to quitting drugs in order to save his relationship—and life. That's how I would like to end the story of Lisa and Rich, but tragically, his valiant effort at sobriety was in vain. A few weeks after leaving rehab, he passed away from necrotizing fasciitis, or flesh-eating disease, due to his weak immune system.

"I had to go back to work two weeks later. Everyone we worked with knew what happened. I hid to avoid people; I was tired of people saying they were sorry for my loss. Management asked the other employees not to question me about it, so instead they'd whisper and stare. I was completely lost, looking for ways to numb the pain. I wanted to talk about it, but felt no one could relate. I was unable to focus on anything positive."

The struggles Lisa went through were only amplified by the sudden passing of her mother from cancer, two weeks after her 61st birthday. Just like Kim earlier in this story, Lisa's mother was her best friend; losing her crushed Lisa's already shattered heart. For every woman who has lost a good mom, it's a deep hurt that never fully heals.

"I wanted to give up on myself many times, but my family was the only thing that kept me sane. I started to not care about myself, and had a pity party in my mind on many occasions. I went to work and sat by myself. I would just cry for hours. I called in sick many times, would drink alone and not answer phone calls or texts."

With the support of her family and friends, her first yoga teacher and the power of meditation, Lisa found a way to push through and keep going. Her father became her closest confidante and she spent seven years single, focused on herself. In the beginning, she was painting and drinking every night as an escape. She had cut herself off from most of the world until a good friend gave her the nudge she needed to truly live again. All he did was ask her one question: "You're not dead, so why are you living your life as if you died?"

That powerful sentence motivated Lisa to reconnect with the world. She began passionately pursuing health and wellness initiatives. She had a well-paying day job at a major automotive company, and filled her free time studying to become a yogi. Lisa invested in her new passion by taking a six-week course in Los Angeles, and spending two months in India. Those experiences permanently changed her.

"In India, I learned a lot about what it truly means to be non-judgmental. Different religions come together to help one another. There was this wealthy Muslim family who gave water every day to a Hindu family living in poverty. It was inspiring to see the community taking care of one another. That feeling is at the heart of my yoga practice."

Lisa had the time and energy to balance both jobs and was doing it successfully, until her main employer fired her for promoting health and wellness at work. She was a loyal, well-liked employee for 21 years and all of a sudden, her steady income was gone.

It was an unexpected blow, but her meditation and yoga practice made it easier to rise right back up again. Within a year, Lisa turned her tough break into a successful yoga studio with a better side job. Her resilience is undeniable. In spite of her past heartbreaks, Lisa even opened her heart to the idea of love again. She finally has the healthy, mutually-supportive relationship that she's always deserved.

"I feel like I hit rock bottom a couple times in my life. Meditation and yoga was my first rise; healthy living became my new addiction. My second rise was the support of my husband. He is amazing. Dan built my confidence back up and taught me to trust again. I got right back out there and began a new career, one I truly enjoy going to each day and my family benefits from tremendously."

Her family has grown as well. When Lisa was possibly overdoing her active lifestyle, she ended up missing her monthly period for two years. She was under the impression that she could never have a child, and accepted that motherhood wouldn't be a part of her future. Shortly after marrying the man she believes was sent to her from her mom, Lisa became pregnant.

"First, it was the yellow rose Dan showed up with on our first date. My mom's favorite color was yellow, and my dad always bought her yellow roses. Then, for me to become pregnant after years of believing that I couldn't, it was the greatest blessing! I told my dad after my first date with Dan. 'He's the one. Mom sent him.' Every day he shows me that it's true."

Lisa is now happily married to a good man who understands her struggles and supports her dreams. She has a healthy, happy son, is a proud stepmom to her sweet stepson, runs a business she loves, and knows that no matter what else happens in her life, she will rise, rise again.

HUMBLE HEROES

I'm a huge fan of Dana, so I was thrilled when she agreed to be a part of *Women Ready to Rise*. We've never met in person, but I follow her anti-bullying organization on social media, as well as the other charitable endeavors she promotes. We bonded immediately over our shared battle against bullying and our advocacy for various social justice issues.

Although she's overcome significant challenges and still battles serious health concerns, Dana gleefully uses every free moment to lift others up. Her ear-to-ear grin and positive energy are contagious online and have gained her a large, loyal following, including several well-known actors. She's also a gifted writer, so I knew putting this section in the book would be a snap. I'll start with the reason Dana is allowing me to share her story, in her own words.

> "Before I say anything, I want it to be known that telling my story and being this open—more vulnerable than I have ever been in my life—is meant to inspire, help, and hopefully motivate others. My ultimate goal is to spread hope to all women, no matter what they are going through or have gone through. I am in no way special. So many women have been through the same, if not worse, in their life. I want people reading this to feel empowered. It is not to feel sorry for me or to pity me in any way at all, because that is not what I want to come out of this, ever."

Empathy, hope and inspiration, *not* pity, is the driving force behind telling all of our stories. Dana knows the power of using her voice to inspire others to speak up for themselves. It's literally the prime purpose of her anti-bullying organization, and how we originally connected. Coincidentally, yet predictably, she has the same motivation as I do. Dana knows what it's like to feel worthless or powerless, and has made it her mission to ensure others feel valuable and powerful. It's a common thread amongst the strongest survivors.

I've known Dana for several years, watched her videos and read her blogs, but only had this general idea that she must have overcome serious struggles to be the person she is today. I knew she was a survivor with a tough medical history, but I didn't know the details of everything she had endured. She is always celebrating the resilience of other survivors like myself, never focusing on her own hardships. Dana knows what she's doing and why she does it.

> "I have, for years, been telling or sharing other survivors' stories, and have really divulged little about myself. I am so used to helping others, I never realized how healing it was to finally release my story and talk about myself. Or the fact of how many people my story could help or inspire. I believe in being a survivor and telling your story from that perspective, not as a victim.
>
> "My focus was always on lifting others, listening to them, putting a smile on my face to make them laugh or feel better, pretending I was fine. I was very good at hiding my emotions and what I was going through, with the exception of a few people who are close to me—and even they do not know the full story. I always felt like nobody was truly listening, or even cared.
>
> "My main concern was making sure nobody else had to go through some of the things I did, or feel the way I did. I do not want to see people in pain. It impacts me, as I believe that I can feel their pain. I guess I have always had such deep empathy for people. I do not want anyone to make the same mistakes I did."

It's interesting that advocates who are lifting others up don't always realize that others will be happy to do the same in return. We're in this world together, and everyone goes through challenges; this book is substantial evidence of that. There is no shame in reaching out for support. Dana would open her arms to anyone who needed a hug. I'm certain there are countless people who want to hold Dana up as well.

She has experienced abuse in every form, including physical abuse, emotional manipulation, and sexual assault from the very adults you are supposed to be able to trust. The worst part is that her experiences were dismissed as nothing, or she was not believed at all—forcing Dana to act as if nothing was wrong.

"The very first time was at a doctors office for my first Pap smear. How he was touching me felt wrong. It didn't seem like it was part of the test. I doubt you check anything by rubbing an area outside of where they are supposed to be examining. I told someone related to me, and she laughed. She said that is not supposed to happen, but nothing was done. I brushed it off as no big deal, because it did not seem to matter to her.

"It was that same relative's alcoholic, cheating husband that touched me and did sexually inappropriate things to me. He molested me. The only reason it never turned into sex is because the night he tried while I was sleeping, he woke me up with his hands up my shirt, touching my breasts. I pretended to sleep; I was frozen. I had to turn over to get it to stop. He continued to try to pull me back on my back, but I kept pushing forward.

"He left after that and went back to bed with a woman who was very close to me at that time. I should have never gone there to stay, because something weird always happened with him. Almost every single time. I always felt guilty, like I allowed it to happen, but I was scared and young. I did not know if it was all in my head, because *everything* was always in my head, according to the adults.

"When I finally got the courage to tell her years later as an adult, she didn't believe me. She later asked him and he denied it. So, I never mentioned it again. I struggled with what happened, but I kept going. It did impact me occasionally when I was affectionate with others. There are triggers that you have to learn how to control, but will still be there to some extent, no matter what you do."

Although the violations of her body at a young age had a traumatic impact, Dana says the verbal, emotional, and mental abuse did the most damage. Although she seemed to dance around the details in her answers to me, it was obvious she was not blessed with a loving and supportive childhood. She recalls being told some very damaging things as a child.

"I heard, 'Why did God give me you as a child? What did I do to deserve this punishment?' And 'I wish I'd never had you,' probably came out once or twice when I was growing up, too."

The lack of love and stability in her upbringing made her next challenge even more difficult. Dana has gone through several health scares, and almost died twice. First it was a rare blood disorder that came with chronic fatigue syndrome, coupled with anemia and mono. Waiting to learn if she had leukemia, lymphoma, or another serious disease that could kill her was terrifying, yet she felt eerily calm about it.

"The anxiety was not even there. Compared to other things I had been through, I found this to be the easiest, because I could finally focus on myself. I thought others would, too. Unfortunately, other people continued their selfish ways, even when I was in and out of the hospital."

Dana was diagnosed with immune thrombocytopenia (ITP), which is a disorder that causes easy or excessive bruising and bleeding. The bleeding results from unusually low levels of platelets, hindering blood clotting.

"I developed a strong faith during the time I was laying there sick. The only ones I knew I could count on were the only ones I really wanted around: my fiancé and the woman who was like a mother figure to me since I was about 17 years old. It eventually ended in surgery, a splenectomy, after transfusions, hospital stays, a long period on steroids, and numerous doctor appointments.

"A few years later, I caught pneumonia and almost died. I made it to the hospital just in time. With no spleen, I have to be very careful. Common illnesses can kill me quite fast. That was another long hospital stay and road to recovery. I was never the same. My body, my mind, my strength... I was completely burnt out. I was too young to die and didn't want to, even though at times I wished I was never born."

Although she didn't have a lasting desire to die at any point, Dana admits the thought seriously toyed with her mind at least once. She was staying in an apartment where the owner had a gun, legally. She had been drinking and was quite depressed at the time. She had never held a gun or loaded one.

"I took one of the bullets out and was curious to see if I could load the gun. I did, and just stared at it for a long time. I was breaking down completely at this point, because the life I envisioned for myself was so out of control.

"After a while I took the bullet out, because my intention was not to die, but to see if I could pull the trigger. What if I was gone? Would anybody even notice or care? That was what I was curious about. Would anybody care, and what legacy would I leave?

"After I took the bullet out, I pulled the trigger. Maybe it was to prove something to myself? I am not really sure why I did it, but I did not want to die. That was dangerous territory for me and a reminder of the strength I had: the fight that was still in me. I meandered into an extremely dark territory that I had never been to before. That night released a truth in me that I now had to deal with, because one's mind should never reach such an extreme point."

I'm personally grateful Dana never pulled that trigger with the bullet inside, and I'm quite confident that I'm not the only one. She has impacted the lives of countless people through her social media posts, supportive outreach efforts, informative articles, and constant encouragement.

The traumatic experiences and abuse that shaped her childhood, accompanied with her serious medical issues, impacted even the strongest of her relationships. Dana fell in love with her best friend at age seventeen and was married at twenty. She was divorced by age twenty-six. She doesn't regret her marriage, even though it didn't last as long as they intended. The separation was mutual, and she still cares for her ex sincerely. However, it was another roadblock she had to find a way to get over, rather than beat herself up over a failed marriage.

A lack of unconditional love and support as a child made it hard for Dana to learn how to love herself unconditionally. When something horrible would happen, she would get lost in an internal debate of whether she deserved it or not. Absolutely no one deserves the verbal abuse, sexual assault, and health problems Dana has faced. The feelings of worthlessness from her childhood kept resurfacing until she realized that she had to forgive those who hurt her, and learn that she is in control of her life.

"Those are some major events that led me to where I am today, and who I am. I got as far away from it all as I could. I ran. I still had to deal with it, though, no matter how far I ran. You can't run away, and I realized that as I got older. To be honest, I still am running from it in some ways, and I am working on changing that. It is a long process to recover from trauma. It doesn't happen overnight, and there is no magic cure or pill.

"After I got tired of always feeling stressed, depressed, and angry, and not living my best life, I just decided to do something about it. So, I made some drastic changes, and here I am. At some point we have to stop feeling sorry for ourselves if we want to help others. I had to not only forgive those who hurt me, but myself as well. I can't stress enough just how important that is to healing.

"I woke up one day and got my shit together. I unpacked my baggage, literally and figuratively, said goodbye to the former love of my life—but still one of my best friends—and embarked on new adventures. I made new, different friends. I delved into new things and discovered my bisexuality. Left old passions behind; left old habits behind. Found new hobbies. Found new light in my heart. New ambitions and new goals. Found hidden parts of myself. Found lost parts of myself."

Although there have been many painful moments in Dana's past, she dug down deep and chose to rise stronger. She tapped into the unconditional love she felt from her grandmothers and a few other loved ones, whom she credits with her resilience.

In spite of the various abuse, medical mysteries, and deadly close calls, Dana has a remarkable list of accomplishments. She earned her degree in psychology with minors in child development and criminal justice. She has a flourishing career working for a large company in the medical field.

Dana started her anti-bullying organization in 2014, where she has partnered with incredible organizations and powerful people to raise awareness of critical social issues. She hosts podcasts and is a red-carpet reporter. As a gifted writer and activist, her work has been published on quite a few prominent websites. Above all the challenges she's overcome and impressive feats she's accomplished, Dana is a humble woman who simply wants to pass the tough lessons she's learned onto others.

"I never really saw myself as a woman ready to rise until I looked back at everything I have been through later in life, and saw how strong I really am. I didn't fail. I made it through, but my work is not done. It's never done. Self-care and love is a lifelong class."

Dana is a woman ready to rise because she has found a purpose for the pain she went through. She dedicates her free time to lifting others up, which in turn keeps her afloat. Even when Dana is at her lowest, she's still trying to help others rise.

I was reviewing Dana's story prior to sending her the final proof to review, and it just happened to be the evening before she had another surgery. Her health had been shaky for several months, and I was curious to see how she was handling everything on social media.

In typical Dana style, she had a post about her gratitude towards anyone who had shown her concern or wished her well, with an adorable photo of her with her tongue sticking out. Her Twitter account was full of World Kindness Day posts, uplifting quotes, and promotions for a passion project on climate change. Her efforts to improve the world around her are evident everywhere, even when she's dealing with her own illness.

Thank you, Dana, for raising us up with you, every time you rise.

My next humble hero crossed my path on social media several years ago. I believe it was our mutual support of Dana's anti-bullying organization that initially brought us together, although it isn't the only place our paths have crossed online. We saw something in each other worth holding onto, and now Kenzie and I are so intermingled on all of our social media that it feels like we must be friends offline as well.

I asked her to be in this book because Kenzie is undeniable proof that you can turn any tragedy into a triumph. She's faced several noteworthy challenges, and is now using the compassion and strength she gained from those difficult experiences to literally save lives. She's been knocked down and out, over and over again, yet always finds the strength to bounce back up.

Kenzie was raised by a father who turned a blind eye to a verbally and physically abusive mother, which later manifested into a feeling of worthlessness and falling for a toxic man. How she was treated in her formative years led to self-destructive behavior, almost to the extreme of taking her own life.

Thankfully, now Kenzie searches for the good in everything, including her parents' missteps. Kenzie made a point of defending her parents' actions after reading the final version of her story, because they did support her financially and are currently trying to make amends after a lengthy period without any communication. Her heart is focused on forgiveness and gratitude, as that's the only way to move forward from her past.

> "Molested as a child, child abuse, both physically and emotionally. My mother had mental health issues that led to violent fits when I was too young to understand what was going on. I had an eating disorder with self-degradation after my own mother told me I was fat and ugly.
> "I knew I was a lesbian, but was raised in a Catholic, Republican household where I was constantly told homosexuality was wrong. I had a boyfriend who raped and abused me. Then, I started dating a girl and my parents found out. I was beaten for my 'sin' and kicked out of the house. I started smoking and drinking, had suicidal ideation with a plan."

Kenzie lists the facts surrounding her troubled childhood as if it was an ordinary grocery list of experiences that everyone must go through. She's not the only participant in this book who did the same, and there's a reason behind it. After writing my first memoir and having to discuss the deeply personal details of the abuse publicly, I had to train myself to do the same. It's a disassociation technique that allows you to contain your emotions when you're talking about something that's truthfully too painful to discuss. This is a much healthier coping method compared to how Kenzie used to deal with her trauma.

> "I was pissed off and started cutting my legs, because it hurt too much on my wrists to cut deeper. I started drinking to take the edge off, and kept cutting my leg. I reached a point where the outer pain overcame my inner pain and was able to distract my thoughts from my wrists. Cutting made everything more tolerable, and that became my coping mechanism."

When Kenzie was self-harming, she was still bulimic, struggling to love herself, and feeling like she was failing at creating the future she deserved.

Cutting herself created physical pain that distracted her from the emotional pain, so she could push forward.

"I remember the day I decided that I didn't want to live anymore. The rape, abuse, losing my first love, being told I was ugly, wrong, and a disappointment... The negative feedback was never-ending. I felt like I couldn't do anything right.

"After the night that my mother showed up at the movie theatre, found me with my girlfriend and beat me in front of her, I broke up with her. I was afraid of what might happen to her if my mother lost control and hurt her. She didn't understand; I broke her heart. We were in the same circle of friends, and I lost all of them. I should have had more courage to stand up for her, for us, but I was young and naïve. I remember not caring about anything after that.

"I couldn't see a future past high school. I stopped doing schoolwork, stopped talking and going to my extracurriculars. I cleaned out my locker and took signs down that the softball team had made me earlier that year. I had a contact that would buy me beer and liquor, so I took some home after everyone was asleep. I ran the water in the bathtub, and turned the lights out except for a candle. I had a knife and a bunch of empty bottles of alcohol next to the tub. I reached the point that I was spinning and thought it was time.

"I heard my phone go off, which I thought was odd because no one ever called me; (this was before texting). It was late, which was even more out of the ordinary. I let it go, and started to cut my wrist. I remember it being painful, though everything else felt numb. I tried to take a deep breath and go faster and deeper, but it was too hard. It made me angry, so I started slashing at my leg. That wasn't as painful. I remember seeing the blood, feeling the burning, and I stopped.

"My phone went off again. I sat there for a few minutes, crying and thinking that I couldn't even do this right. I held toilet paper against the cuts until they stopped bleeding, wrapped them with Coband, and got out of the tub.

"My phone went off again. I had three missed calls and a voicemail from one of the instructors at the softball facility. She hadn't heard from me in a few weeks, and hadn't seen me around the gym. She knew I may be busy with school, but something was telling her to check on me. She told me that she loved and cared about me. I didn't call her back that night. I can't describe the feeling I had at that moment. This woman wasn't one of my closest friends, and yet she felt like she needed to check on me."

Kenzie wasn't meant to end her life in the tub that day; she had a future to create. She had a talent and passion for softball, so she decided to refocus her energy on becoming good enough to make a Division One team. Her efforts paid off with an athletic scholarship, and she became a starter after a brief trial period. She was trying for a sense of normalcy. Unfortunately, her eating disorder and cutting were noticeably affecting her ability to excel.

"My coaches noticed a decrease in my performance and confronted me about my eating disorder. I was warned that I wouldn't play if I didn't get my life together. Thankfully, they helped by offering resources for my recovery.

"I was injured during my junior year, and my performance was nowhere what it should have been. The doctors gave me medications for pain and inflammation to get through practices and games. I received epidural steroid injections that failed. I developed a tolerance to the narcotics and slowly increased the doses past the recommended values. I didn't realize I was also creating an addiction.

"Once I graduated, the healthcare stopped—and so did the pills. I had to detox on my own at my apartment, not really understanding what was happening. I spent two weeks in my apartment throwing up, shaking, breaking things, and contemplating suicide again."

Thankfully for us, Kenzie didn't end her life in those fleeting moments of hopelessness, otherwise she wouldn't be saving lives now as an emergency medivac paramedic. This woman rose from wishing she would die to literally saving lives, one brave step at a time.

Of course, she still had a few more hills to climb before landing her dream job, like her first boss sexualizing her every chance he got.

> "While I was in grad school, I worked as an administrative assistant and my boss was absolutely disgusting. He would make comments about my breasts, my body, my ass."

I don't even want to guess how many women reading the description of her boss' behavior can relate to it. Kenzie hated her job and was struggling in her college courses due to the concussions she suffered. It became an internal struggle each day to keep going. Thankfully, she met a woman, quit school and moved to where her girlfriend lived. Her girlfriend wanted to be a nurse, so since she couldn't find work in teaching, Kenzie decided to venture down the same path.

> "When I first started, they asked me my goal and I said it was to be on the helicopter. They laughed, and said, 'Everyone wants that and no one ever gets on the helicopter, so you should probably focus on just being a nurse right now.'
>
> "Eventually I became a very capable nurse, then oriented into trauma and was one of the nurses on the core trauma committee. I went back to EMT school, took the test to become a paramedic, and found a part time job for experience.
>
> "Eventually, I tested for my current company in medivac helicopter services, both pre-hospital and critical care. I still have a long way to go and am constantly learning. I have repeatedly been

told I would never be able to do something, which gave me the motivation I needed to prove them wrong and do what I wanted."

Warrior woman! Through no actions of her own, Kenzie's life was on the wrong path right from birth. By her own actions and fierce determination, she found a way to redirect it towards the life she deserves. When people told her that she couldn't do something she wanted, she viewed it as a challenge. She believed in herself and persevered. Now, she's using that same fighting spirit to help every patient who crosses her path.

"There are always calls that you remember in the field. Working as a nurse on the helicopter, you see a lot of things—but your time with the patients is so limited, due to the urgency of the calls and the time you have in flight. You're always pushed for shorter times and higher numbers in any field.

"There was one time I got called for a rape victim who was suicidal. My partner and I spent almost an hour trying to help her. Our phones were blowing up with calls from dispatch, and the shift commander was asking why we were on scene so long. He said we needed to move or cancel.

"This was a call that hit close to home for me. We called our shift commander back, who yelled at us. My partner and I had a momentary breakdown out of frustration. We cried and relived our own nightmares. We decided that we had done the right thing and didn't care what management had to say about it. There are reasons we are in this profession and it isn't for numbers. If we can't help the patients that actually need it, then we are not the service that should be taking these calls.

"The ones that hit the most are the child abuse cases, shaken baby syndrome victims who have brain hemorrhages and depressed skull fractures. The ones you hold in the dark trying to soothe because they are in so much pain and don't understand that crying increases their intracranial pressure, making the pain worse. The ones that you perform CPR on for countless minutes trying to bring them back. The ones who die with no family by their side, because they have already been arrested or can't be found. The countless rape kits you perform where you try to be compassionate, but also desensitize yourself so it doesn't impact you personally.

"The suicide calls you pick up that you know aren't viable, but you try your hardest anyway. I can't imagine the pain they had to be in to follow through, and what they will have to endure if they survive. These thoughts go to the back of your head as you pour blood into these people, administer medications, drill for lines, drop tubes into tracheas, strap down tourniquets, apply countless gauze pads and towels to stop bleeding, squeeze the bag to make them breathe.

"You don't think about it until afterwards. You cope with whatever means you need. Some people run or work out, some hit a punching bag or down a bottle. Some people develop a dark sense of humor that only those like you would understand. I'm grateful for the family I've made in my workplace.

"If I had known what I know now as a teenager when I wanted to end my life, the thought would have never crossed my mind. I've seen the aftermath it causes. I've seen the regret, pain, and confusion. I've seen people recover who said they should have never done it. If I had known the support I would have now and the great things there are in life, I never would have considered it.

"Just because you feel all alone at one point doesn't mean you are, or that you won't find people later. That's why it is important to be kind and offer assistance to people when you can. It may make them stop for one second and rethink their decision. I learned that I am so much more than what I've been told or what I believed. People are alive because of me. If I had taken my own life, they may not have had the same outcome."

She fought the urge to give up when she was at her lowest, and now she fights for the lives of strangers in her job every day. That's a hero. That's a person with purpose. Kenzie's life was an uphill battle, but she still found a way to succeed. If Kenzie can rise above all those who tried to tear her down, so can you.

RISING ABOVE THE GLASS CEILING

This chapter honors two trailblazing women who've broken through male-dominated industries and created their own successful businesses. I'm blessed to know many impressive female entrepreneurs and executives through a local group, Windsor Women in Business. It was founded by this positive ball of energy named Natalie, whom I instantly admired. Although she isn't featured in this book, she's another exemplary example of a woman ready to rise.

I met my super supportive friend Sheryl (and several other women in this story) at a Windsor Women in Business social, and we quickly clicked. She's a take-no-nonsense woman with a fighting spirit and a huge heart. I was drawn into her energy and had to know more about her.

For most of the other participants, I was aware of the specific challenges they overcame before asking for their involvement in this book. Sheryl was the exception; that's because she's quite exceptional. I assumed that she must have endured difficulties because of the rock-solid success story she is today. Strong people are built through challenging life experiences.

Sheryl is a local business leader in a highly competitive industry who has been busting through ceilings for decades. Her strong work ethic, compassion for others, and calm nature were proof enough that she must have survived her share of storms. When I asked for her involvement, Sheryl knew exactly why she belonged in this story.

"I have been in the business world as a 'little' but powerful female for over forty-five years. I was a part of the movement that saw more women entering the workforce."

Powerful captures both her accomplishments and her perspective. Sheryl was born into an ambitious family, which taught her the value of work and relationships at a young age. She was an only child of two young parents who made sure Sheryl was never spoiled. Her father and grandfather ran a family-owned business that her grandfather had started when he emigrated from the Russian/Turkish border in the early 1920s.

"After escaping under the cloak of night, he fled Communism and persecution and landed in Canada as a refugee. He was sent to Saskatchewan, where he worked in the fields until he 'graduated' to working in the farmer's general store. Grandpa met my grandma and moved to Windsor, opened the store, and lived to be 102! He was a huge role model, and I was incredibly fortunate to have him well into my adult life."

Sheryl has her grandfather's spunk. She's willing to leap the hurdles and make the tough decision to keep pursuing her path. Her decades of success in sales, marketing, and publishing were fostered by the solid work ethic she was shown as a kid.

"I was taught to always give 100%, not be judgmental, and to treat customers the way I would want to be treated. Patience, skill, good manners, and respect for others was the mantra of the business world I was competing in."

This most certainly describes Sheryl, but her genuine professionalism is accompanied with a bit of a defiant side. A perfect example of her independent ways is how she answered two of my most essential questions for this book. I asked every woman in this book how they felt at their lowest point, and how they were able to rise after hitting rock bottom.

"I don't believe I've had a lowest point. I was taught that you get up, you be positive, put your best foot forward, and you do the best you can do. I don't believe that I ever hit rock bottom. My resilience and practical nature allowed me to rise above the low points, and made me even more determined to be a success at what I did."

Sheryl, like my mother and most women born in the 20th century, was raised not to talk about her problems. Women didn't want to be pitied, so everyone kept everything inside. In the last ten or twenty years, we have begun to realize that not sharing our stories leads to inequality, unreported cases of domestic abuse and rape, and undiagnosed mental illnesses, all of which could end in suicide. Too many secrets lurk behind closed doors. It's why we must speak up now, and the purpose behind this very book.

Sheryl hasn't faced any of the above, as far as I know, but her life hasn't been without its own challenges. She and her husband found a way to survive and start over when they were suddenly unemployed with a baby, living in high-priced Toronto.

"I have had a life that has been fulfilling, both personally and throughout my career. I spent twenty-two years in the china, crystal, and home furnishings industry, as one of the leading experts in the country. In 1992, the industry downsized itself as social demographics and the Toronto economy changed, and I lost a job I loved. My son was a year old and my husband John and I were both in the same boat, unemployed in the same industry, living the life on the 42nd floor of a Toronto high-rise."

Being young parents with no income, living in one of the most expensive cities in Canada, must have been terrifying. The panic of the situation didn't seem to rattle Sheryl or John. At a time when most people would be scared to spend, let alone borrow any money for a risky venture, Sheryl went all in.

"I found the Wedding Guide, a franchise from Denver, and knew right away it was for me. However, we had to find the money for the franchise fee. Banks not only weren't keen on lending money to a new small business, they were definitely hesitant in providing loans to a woman in an industry I knew nothing about. I was refused by many traditional lenders, and finally found a male banker at a small T.D. bank branch in Leaside who consented to provide me with the $25,000 I needed."

From my perspective, that was the moment Sheryl rose. It may not have been what she thinks of rock bottom, but she was at a point where she could either wallow in the fact that she was jobless, or rise above the roadblock by turning it into a lucrative opportunity. Thankfully, Sheryl chose the latter.

"That first year, I paid back the loan, lost twenty-five pounds while working hard, and delivered the first and most profitable issue ever in the history of the Wedding Guide's 100 other franchises. That record was never broken. It was a glorious accomplishment, and I knew that I had made the right decision. It's 26 years later, and I have never looked back! I love what I do!"

She took a chance, worked her ass off and was rewarded. That's a pretty powerful example of turning what could be a tragedy into a triumph, and it only gets better. Four years later, Sheryl and her family made another bold decision to move back to her hometown of Windsor.

"It was an amazing experience to restart the same business in a different trading area and to raise our then-four-year-old son where he had grandparents, and a great-grandfather who lived to be 102. I felt it was time to give back, and it was one of the best decisions that we made together."

Sheryl is passionate about her family and the Wedding Guide, as well as the city of Windsor. She's vocal about the reputation and quality of care for businesses in our city's downtown core. She's regularly active in promoting local entrepreneurs, and has immersed herself in efforts to celebrate the Windsor community.

"Windsor also gave me the opportunity to get into the music business as one of the organizers of Bluesfest International, which I was proudly part of for 18 years. Long lasting friendships were made, and I learned a completely new business. This also spawned being one of the founding members of the Canada South Blues Society and the Canada South Festival Network, where I volunteered for over five years. I was very proud to receive an Ontario Volunteer award in 2004 and a recognition award from the Network. Today I receive great pleasure from meeting and mentoring entrepreneurial women who are inspiring to me with their passion and resolve to do great things with their businesses."

That's the fierce leader I know her to be, and the reason I asked her to be in this story. I make a point of scheduling a dinner date with Sheryl a few times a year, so I can soak up as much of her wisdom as possible. She is this tiny but mighty force, giving others the confidence to stand tall and pursue their passions.

"I urge everyone to follow their dreams and try new things. I'm curious and inquisitive. I've learned how to be bold and fair, and that it's OK to ask for what I need. I found courage in sharing my convictions and understand how important it is to strike a balance in life. I love to read, cook, and share quality time with friends. Friendship means a lot to me, as does a hearty topic of conversation to chew on.

"My life's experiences—being a businesswoman in a man's world, a ten-year marriage beginning at nineteen, a mother late in life, and a wife to a man who stole my heart over three decades ago—have brought me to this time and place that reassures me that all of the hard work and decision making was correct. We can meet our challenges head on, or we can run and hide. Struggles continue to manifest themselves until you deal with them."

Sheryl blazed a trail, easing the burden on all those who follow. Her journey had its share of roadblocks and unexpected turns, but she kept going. Sheryl was determined to rise and achieved success because she never gave up. It's an example every woman should follow.

The next generation of entrepreneurial women are grateful to women like Sheryl, for making it a little easier to break through the glass ceiling. I'm extremely fortunate when it comes to lasting friendships, and Rahel is another one of my best friends of over twenty years. In spite of her answer to the first question I asked every participant (Why do you think I asked you to be in this book?), our forever friendship is not the reason she was so high on my list.

"Because I am your best friend...duh! LOL.

"You know everything about me, and know that life hasn't always been easy, but most of all because I am a dreamer. I come up with ideas and inspiration to make big moves and take risks. I'm not happy living a stagnant life with no real excitement or adventure. I need challenges to overcome and goals to crush.

"I am where I am today because of all the various risks I took in life, and crazy dreams I've followed so passionately. Sure, I have failed at some of my attempts and ideas, but I either tried again or came up with a new plan. To me, it's all about calculated risks and coming up with a solid action plan to make it happen."

Rahel has experienced many of the same struggles and successes as Sheryl, and she's still fighting daily to claim her stake in a male dominated industry. In fact, that battle consumes the majority of her sleeping hours and was the reason Rahel holds the record for taking the longest time to answer my questions for this story (approximately two years). Luckily, I knew she'd be worth the wait.

"My latest adventure has been starting my own business, where I can work from home and still have a respectable career. I have taken the skills I've learned from working as a designer in the automotive industry and turned them into a freelancing business that is thriving. This was no easy feat."

Rahel is a 3D fixture designer, something she's repeatedly explained to me and I still don't fully comprehend. Using complex software, Solid Works, she creates three-dimensional images (like a blueprint) of various automotive and industrial components. Mechanical Techniques - CAD/CAM was the program she studied in college, and she landed a great job after graduation in her field. Shortly afterward, she became pregnant with her first daughter and married her high school sweetheart in a tropical paradise.

Her career path was off to a fantastic start—until the economy in Windsor took a drastic turn for the worse. The local automotive industry collapsed in 2008, and gainful employment was suddenly quite scarce. Financial stability was essential for their new family, so they began searching for opportunities outside of their hometown.

"With the fate of the automotive industry in limbo, my husband Chris and I decided this was our opportunity to seek employment outside of Windsor and escape the city. Since both of us were employed in the auto industry, we felt that everything we've worked so hard for was in jeopardy. I was pregnant at the time with our second child, and we put our house on the market with no clear path of where we were going.

"Chris started looking for work as a machinist anywhere in Canada, which led us to several opportunities. Shortly after having our daughter, we moved our young family seven hours away from everyone and everything we'd ever known. With all of the excitement of this new adventure, I never expected to feel so empty after moving away."

Her husband would make enough money that she could afford to stay home with her girls, something Rahel truly wanted to do while they were still young. They quickly packed up their home and moved their family first into a rental property, and the following year into their permanent home, tucked deep inside a serene forest.

"I was on maternity leave when we moved away from Windsor, and life was full of new experiences as we settled into our new location and home. I was truly excited for this new chapter of my life, but within a few months of moving, I became depressed. I have conquered depression in my life before, but this time it was different. I didn't have my family and friends to surround myself with and share some of my struggles. I felt like I had no one but my husband and two little girls.

"I had become a stay-at-home mom and I was living in the middle of nowhere. My life did a complete turnaround from living in the city with a promising career. I felt so confused. Moving away was something I was *so* excited about, but after completing the mission, I was anything but happy."

Although I know she's never regretted their decision, the sheer distance from her family and friends has been a challenge since she left Windsor. I personally think it sucks that I'm not able to hug Rahel through the phone when I know she's having a rough time. The first few years were filled with many of those moments while she adjusted to being a stay-at-home mother of two little ones and a hyperactive puppy.

With time, Rahel developed a routine and loved her new home life. However, the lack of interaction with the outside world left her feeling lonely. Her house was almost an hour outside of the closest city, there are not any community groups she could get involved in, and she missed earning her own paycheck. Once both her girls were in school full time, the urge to re-enter the workforce became too much to ignore. Unfortunately, there was no one in the area hiring in her field.

"Living out in the middle of nowhere made me feel like I had less job opportunities. The fact that there are no machine shops in my area that could utilize my skills—and I had taken off over five years to raise my two girls—made me scared shitless to re-enter the workforce. What the hell was I going to do?

"With both of the girls going to school full-time, I needed to find a different way to feel valuable to myself and my family. Staying at home to clean all day was totally not satisfying for me, but I didn't know what to do. This led me down several paths before I figured out my calling.

"Instead of relying on a company to give me a job, I created my own. I had valuable skills that I was anxious to use again, and with no job opportunities for my field in this area, I got creative and offered my skills to everyone online."

Rahel tried freelance writing from home at first, but the money was unstable and it didn't give her the outside connections she craved. She's a fantastic baker and eventually found part-time work at a bakery, but the hourly wage was never enough to make an impact on their family expenses. During her job searches, Rahel discovered there was a definite demand for 3D fixture designers, just no existing company willing to fulfill the need.

She invested thousands in retraining, as there had been several significant software advancements, and built a brand-new business from concept to reality.

"My first challenge to overcome was making a name for myself and getting companies to give me a chance. Not only was I trying to sell them on my skills, I was also trying to sell them on the idea of outsourcing their design work to a complete stranger. Someone who could potentially have no idea what they are doing, or just leave them high and dry when things get tough.

"To make things even more challenging, I was trying to do all of this remotely, as there are no machine shops in my area that could use my skill set. So, with the power of the internet and a lot of persistence, I slowly started to bring in some design work.

"Chris and I had this dream that he would someday be able to join me and work from home too. So, after some careful thought, and much contemplation, we decided to call our business CR Fixture Design. We had a five-year plan in mind, that if we worked hard, he would be able to leave his full-time career as a machinist and join the design world.

"Within a year and a half, we had companies knocking down our door, seeking out our services. We had to make a quick decision: either turn away a bunch of work, or find someone to help me get these designs done. This was our moment. It came a lot sooner than we had expected, but this was our time to put our money where our mouth is and go for it. We made the decision that it was finally time for Chris to quit his stable, full-time career and take our future into our own hands. Super scary!!"

One of the advantages of sharing Rahel's story is that I remember these moments in detail. We talk every week for an hour, so I know how nervous that leap was for her family. She and her husband are still taking on side jobs like snow plowing and property management to diversify their portfolio, so they're never stuck without work. They've been working six or seven days a week, ten to fourteen hours a day, for the past year to keep up with the demand.

There are still challenges, like chasing clients on the other side of the border for past due payments, intense conference calls with big players in the automotive and aerospace industries, and being parents to two highly active, ambitious girls. Rahel also struggles with anxiety.

"I have always had some level of anxiety, and a bit of O.C.D., but the anxiety really crept up around the time I started working at the bakery. Instead of just taking some pills like the doctor suggested, I sought out a therapist. She helped me see where my issues were creeping up from and how to overcome the feeling that I wasn't good enough. I still get panic attacks, especially when I feel overwhelmed with work and then look around at my messy house. I am learning to deal with it and prioritize the tasks that need to get done. I find that writing lists and learning to let go of the small things makes a huge difference."

Rahel is currently sacrificing a social life and relaxation, but she is already working on strategies to incorporate a little more down time. That's the cost of a new business. Success takes work, but it's worth it when you're pursuing a life you love. Rahel loves working at home with the love of her life by her side, and appreciates having the flexibility to be involved in everything her kids are doing.

"Happiness is what motivated me. I was not happy with my life and wanted to do better things. It took me awhile to figure out what the missing pieces were. It's still not perfect, but working on making the picture whole is an amazing feeling. Talking to friends and family who supported my dreams and ideas was key."

I'm proud to be one of those friends who cheered this venture on, and sincerely appreciate that she took the time to give me such inspiring answers for this book. She may have taken the longest to submit her response, but Rahel's story took the least time to write. I was blessed to watch her smash through the glass ceiling and build a solid, highly-technical business, and now I'm honored to share Rahel's journey to the top with you.

HEALTH IS EVERYTHING

The next warrior woman I'm honored to introduce was recommended for this book by a woman I trust with my life, my lifelong friend Rahel. I met Leonora at a party I went to with Rahel nearly twenty years ago, when we were still young, dumb, and ready to set the world on fire. None of us had any clue what our futures would hold.

The future Leonora was trying so hard to create for herself was shattered in a matter of seconds when she was only 36. All of her ambitious plans to climb the corporate ladder had to suddenly be put on indefinite hold. There was something more important than her career or even her kids that required her immediate attention: her health. Leonora was diagnosed with metastatic breast cancer.

Those six letters change everything.

> "From the diagnosis to how to share your cancer news with your loved ones and friends, from going through a mastectomy to chemotherapy treatments and losing your hair, it felt like I had to sacrifice a huge part of myself to get better."

Shortly after her diagnosis, Leonora went through a partial mastectomy, removing her right breast. Her recovery from the surgery was fairly bearable, so she continued studying and acing tests, praying she could continue slaying her goals. She did what needed to be done, and was ready to put her life back on track.

Leonora is a practicing Christian who chooses to focus on her blessings and maintain a positive attitude, regardless of life's inevitable challenges. Her faith kept her spirits up during the initial chaos. As strong as her faith may be, it couldn't alleviate the physical pain and exhaustion that chemotherapy inevitably brings.

"Chemotherapy was *the* most frustrating: a complete mind boggle. I would receive treatment and the side effects would last for nine days straight! On the day before my next chemotherapy treatment, I would get one good day when the side effects subsided.

"Although I was very weak, I made sure to step outside regardless of the weather and admire nature, getting fresh air and the opportunity to walk without assistance. It seems small, but it meant so much to me!

"Imagine spending nine days of constant pain, fainting, dizzy spells, and worse. There were lots of times I wanted to give up. I told myself I had the right to feel how I needed to feel in that moment, but then I would let it go. I didn't hold onto those dark thoughts, because the further you think about it, the easier you can reach a point of no return. Thoughts are powerful, and I had to find a way to persevere."

Persevering for a person with cancer doesn't look the same as it does for someone who's healthy. Her dreams of managing school during chemotherapy ended up not being realistic. Leonora had to readjust her priorities.

"I was working on a marketing degree from university, but I had to give up my schooling. I thought I would study and correspond while under treatment, but that never happened. I was so *tired* all the time. Giving up my job was also very difficult to do. I was doing well in my career, and to have it suddenly taken away from me, due to an illness outside of my control, made me so upset."

Even if you hate your job, there is not a soul alive who would trade going to work every day for cancer and chemotherapy. Leonora genuinely

loved her role at a retirement living facility, and recently went back to
school with the goal of advancing into a leadership position on their sales
and marketing team. She cried when she made the decision to resign from
her program. Of course, her perspective has changed since then.

"In retrospect, the things that I once thought were important
are no longer important to me. I didn't go back to pursuing my
education to climb the corporate ladder, because I wanted to do
something that was more Leonora, personified. I wanted to give
back to others. I created my www.glow-with-leo.com website and
social media pages, and I am now helping others who are on their
own cancer journey."

Inspiring others with her story is important to Leonora. Her husband,
who she's been with for almost twenty years, truly matters to her. Her son
and daughter are her top priorities. Her family, her friends, and her dogs
complete her life. Staying healthy and cancer-free for those she loves is now
her greatest goal in life. Everything else is expendable.

I'm ecstatic to report that Leonora's health has improved!

"After treatments, I find the real path to wellness is the after
part. You are learning to start all over, and trying to define where
you see yourself and where you want to go. You rethink your values.
I am under close watch for life: tests for life when appropriate. So
far, it's pretty good. They say the first five years after treatments is
a sensitive time, so I am watched closely. Going to appointments
used to annoy me, but now I appreciate it.

"I trust and hope that I will be able to say, 'Having cancer once
is enough.' I hope that what I went through was enough, that I
won't go through it again. You never know, but I always say, you
are stronger than you think."

As if having cancer wasn't enough for Leonora to have to manage,
there's another reason she's a shining example of how women can handle

anything. Leonora is a military wife whose husband is gone all over the world, for months at a time. She moved away from her family to be near the Air Force Base, and doesn't have family support in close proximity. When she was recovering from cancer and chemo, Leonora was also pulling off double parenting duty.

When I invited the women to meet for the cover photo shoot, Leonora's husband was away for six months in Africa. I can't imagine the person you love and depend on being so far away for so long, yet Leonora only touched on it briefly in one of her original answers. I had to ask her about it to get the full story. This is normal life for Leonora; she doesn't see how it makes her even more extraordinary.

"My strength comes from my family values. My maternal grandparents, who barely spoke English, moved from the Philippines to Canada in 1976. They instilled the hard work ethic within their seven children, which they've also instilled within me. My grandmother remained in the old country for one year with six of her kids while my grandfather and his eldest daughter moved to Canada.

"In order for them to bring the rest of my family abroad, my grandfather and aunt had to work and reside in Canada for one year. Any time Cameron leaves for long periods because of his career in the military, I gather my strength from my grandmother. If she can be away from her husband for a full year on her own with six children, surely I can manage being on my own with two children while my husband is away for three to nine months at a time, even though it occurs every year-and-a half.

"I work, a full-time career. The children have extracurricular activities after school. I'm writing a book, keeping up with my blog, and squeezing in workouts to maintain my health. Sometimes it gets lonely, with your other half being somewhere across the world in the arms of danger, but I challenge myself to do the things that I can do in a day—and not to worry about the things that haven't been done yet. I need to pace myself at a level where I feel like I've done my best, I've done good. If my grandparents are countries apart with no means of communication, at least my husband I can FaceTime, despite the different time zones. I appreciate that.

"I was still going through cancer treatments when Cameron had to go to Iraq, leaving me alone with our two children. I didn't know how I was going to be able to get through this one. I had just finished chemotherapy, but I needed a year-and-a-half treatment cycle of Herceptin—which meant carrying on the less invasive treatment and appointments without my husband. He had his call of duty.

"There have been plenty of times I have been in the position of dual parenting, and it wasn't always easy. I had to be the mom and dad, though no one can replace him. It's hard. I couldn't play or build toys with my children. I made sure they did their homework and were fed, had clean clothes, put to bed in a timely manner...you know, life. My grandparents made it work with what they had, teaching me the same.

"As a wife married to a serving member, whom I have known and loved for twenty years, I have chosen this military lifestyle. And that's exactly what it is, a lifestyle. One that I may never ever understand at times, one that puts me in a position to cry, feeling upset or confused. Yet I remain strong, hopeful, and proud. Although I haven't chosen to have cancer, it too has made me cry, feeling upset and confused, but it too has made me stronger, hopeful, accomplished, and has taught me to live again."

Leonora no longer worries about the trivial ups and downs of daily life, because she knows she's an unyielding survivor.

"I've survived my husband going away on long, extensive tours almost every other year. I've survived dealing with life's difficulties, be it people, work, things, or whatever. Once you've had the big C, you don't sweat the small stuff."

Well, ain't *that* the truth!

Everyone's life has some unpleasant shit in it. If you have your health, you have everything. There is nothing more life-changing than dealing with the realistic possibility that your life could legitimately end at any moment. Leonora's health has improved and she's currently cancer-free, but the word itself destroys any hope of immortality.

Quite interestingly, the thought of death inspires us to live. So many women in this book lost people who were incredibly close to them. As tragic as that felt in the moment, losing their loved one inspired them to live their lives to the fullest.

Almost losing her own life brought out the best in Leonora.

"Of course, nobody wants to hear the dreaded C word, but through my being positive, through grace, support from friends, family, and my faith, it has allowed me to grow into the person that I was meant to become. To love, inspire, and encourage those who are going on their incredible personal journey on this little planet we call Earth. That it is not how you start, it is how you finish."

The next woman certainly understands that concept! She has risen from physical challenges since before she was old enough to realize what she was doing. Evie is legally blind. That initial hurdle meant she had to accept at a young age that there would always be things she couldn't do on her own. As a young adult, it made establishing her independence a whole lot trickier.

"Starting life out this way and traveling my unique path has set me up from a very early age to advocate for myself. I learned very young to ask for what I needed, when I needed it. As an adult, this has served me incredibly well. I see so many people who are afraid to ask for help. People are admired if they appear to have 'pulled themselves up by their own bootstraps.' The truth is that no one does anything alone. Everything is connected. In this way, my disability has given me a huge advantage."

Reading through the proud and concise answers she sent for this story confirmed this assertion. I didn't have to tell Evie that she was a woman ready to rise. Evie told me. From as early on as she can remember, she knew her life was unavoidably more difficult than most, and she had already dug deep enough to realize there was strength in her struggles.

"I think you asked me to be in this book because you see me. You see the reality of my story, that there has been struggle after struggle, and that through it, I have always made the choice to rise. Shit, as they say, makes great fertilizer...and boy, do I have a lot of shit."

Like so many other women in this book, Evie recognizes that it was the toughest moments in her life that brought out the best in her. Her disability was only one of the small hurdles she found a way to get over. Growing up, Evie's house was not always a great place to be; she recalls toxic moments from her childhood in vivid detail.

"I grew up not really knowing my dad. We had a good relationship until I was about seven years old; that's when the anger started. I remember one outburst before then that involved throwing a dining room chair across the room and him storming out, leaving my mother to clean up the mess in tears. I don't know how that was ever resolved."

After moving away for her father's job at age nine, the family moved back again three years later and her father began traveling for work. He was gone for weeks, sometimes even months, at the time. He drifted away from the family, first emotionally and then physically. When her dad returned, he was angry and explosive.

"When I think of my dad, I think of beer, cigarettes and anger. When he wasn't drinking, or exhausted, or away on business for months and years at a time, he was a generous, intelligent man, but those memories are few and far between. If I think about it, I can count them on one hand.

"He brought me to a strip club sometime in my twenties and paid for lap dances for me. It was awkward as fuck. He kept handing me money to tip the dancers. It didn't feel right; these weren't the kind of memories I wanted with my dad.

"I remember holes punched in walls, and that moment when you always knew this wasn't going to end before something got broken. He never hit us, but we always lived in fear of it—at least, I know my mom and I did. She has told me many times that she is afraid of him.

"He worked hard to provide a life for us, I'll give him credit for that. I have no debt from my university education because of his diligence, but another thing I don't have is a relationship with him. I value my schooling, but money doesn't make up for memories.

"I have been my mom's confidante for years, through anger and outbursts, fights and frustration. At some point, I realized that by doing this, I was enabling her to stay with a man that she needed to leave. I had to stop.

"The most recent incident includes her showing up at my door at 1:30 a.m. in hysterics because one of my dad's drunken friends tried to rape her in her own bed, ostensibly with my blind drunk dad's permission. My mom lived with me for four months, and just when I thought she might be ready to leave him for good, she went back."

Growing up in an unstable home leaves lasting trauma, but it shouldn't permanently impact you as an adult. There comes a point where we can no longer blame our parents or lose ourselves in an attempt to resolve their issues. Instead, we can learn from their mistakes and build a better future for ourselves. Evie gets it!

"I learned a lot from him about who I do and do not want to be. I stopped drinking this year. I have the occasional beer or wine, but alcohol no longer has a place of importance in my life. I have seen what it can do to a life, to relationships: the collateral damage it wreaks on everyone around the addict. I don't want that for my children.

"I have learned that I can stand on my own, that DNA is not destiny, and that family can be chosen. I am not my past, though it has created me. I am who I decide to be based on what I do at every moment."

She knows how she's grown and benefited from the hardest moments of her life. She's aware that every challenge she faced gave her the strength to endure the next. Evie grew up as the daughter of an alcoholic, experienced depression in her teenage years and postpartum depression after having her son; each obstacle preparing her for what lies ahead.

"In postpartum I felt hopeless, empty, without self or direction. I was ready to die because I wasn't really living. Sitting on the floor of my son's nursery, sleep deprived, my identity shattered, listening to him crying in his crib, and me having no idea how to make any of it stop.

"One of the first things I did was read a book called *Momma Zen: Walking the Crooked Path of Motherhood,* by Karen Maezen Miller that made me feel less alone and less insane. Following that I read *Hand Wash Cold: Care Instructions for an Ordinary Life*, by the same author. The lesson I took from these pages was to reconnect to the ordinary things in life. That I was not above the mundanities of everyday life. That an ordinary, everyday life is a miracle, and that there is joy at the bottom of a dirty kitchen sink, if only you can take the time and make the effort to uncover it. I started by doing my dishes.

"I *hated* dishes. The inevitability of their return made me feel like it was utterly pointless to engage in washing them at all. And so, I started to make short lists of things to do, including my dishes, and trained myself to start feeling good again by checking off one small thing at a time and reveling in that small joy. My dishes became a source of peace and contentment for me. I could always rely on them to accumulate and give me the opportunity to uncover the small happiness that was hiding at the bottom of the pile.

"From there, I started to make friends. I started to read again. I took baby step after baby step every day. I started to meditate daily, journal occasionally, workout regularly. Little by little, I started to feel more at ease, more of the time. I hit the wall of course, as we all do, and got involved in a coaching program. It changed my life. She tore off my blinders, called me on my bullshit, and invited me to grow into my potential. She tore off excuses and blocks I didn't even know I had.

"When the shit hits the fan, as it inevitably will, I have the tools to handle it."

In her honest answer, she shares several great tips on how to manage or move past depression. The first is reading books just like the one you're reading now, that remind you that you're not alone. Other people have experienced similar pain and survived; you will too.

The next essential piece of advice is taking your recovery in baby steps. Whether it is postpartum depression, anxiety, or an emotional trauma, you can't expect to snap your fingers and everything is better. That's where her third point comes in, reaching out for help or motivation. Life is a long, rocky journey, filled with rough terrain. Sometimes you need a coach to guide you through.

Of course, Evie still battles with her anxiety and bouts of self-doubt like most of us, but she's determined not to let circumstances dictate her future. From learning how to navigate the world with limited vision to sharing her unique view of the world through her stories, Evie has continuously found ways to rise above her environment or afflictions. I absolutely love how she owns her accomplishments, because she knows she earned every one.

"I have been published in multiple publications, have a steadily growing blog audience, and have written my first book. I am a newly enamored devotee of Kundalini yoga, and I am not nearly done growing."

When she grew tired of losing retail job opening after opening, due to her visual limitations, she chose to start her own business. She couldn't find an open door, so she created one. Evie is an author, freelance editor, and writing guru. She pens a deeply personal blog that addresses mental health, and creative outlets based on her beautifully forthcoming feelings.

"I have always known, deep inside of me, that I was meant for something bigger. I have always been a bit odd, not quite in sync with the world around me. Knowing deeply that I was called to some meaningful work was what kept me going. It was also, paradoxically, what made the low spots so incredibly hard. If I was meant for something bigger, why was I falling so low?"

The gut feeling that there is greater purpose for our pain is an effective way to get through the toughest times. I tell myself the same thing. Hope is powerful. It reminds us that anything is possible, and brighter days are ahead. Evie is bursting with hope, and that energy is creating the bright future she deserves.

"I have been involved in the writing and editing for six different published authors, and have helped over twenty women create roadmaps for their content that are aligned with their own deep message, and the needs of the people they are dedicated to helping."

Evie is using her skills to elevate other women, while growing a substantial home-based business. She's pursuing her passion and helping others. That's not only the dream of every aspiring writer, it's the primary life pursuit for most people.

> "My struggles have shaped me. Like gold doesn't become beautiful until it has been through the fire, so a person is refined, shined, and beautified through trial, struggle, challenge, loss, and grief."

Whether you can relate to Leonora's sudden life-altering diagnosis or the additional obstacles Evie has managed since birth, any serious health concern is terrifying. Fear and stress is a natural part of the process; so is learning how to cope with whatever your illness might be. I'm grateful these amazing women are thriving, and am certain you have the same ability they do.

MIND OVER MATTER

Mind over matter usually refers to using your mental strength to overcome challenges, but for this chapter, I would like to flip the script. What if everything looks simple and straightforward on paper, but the mind itself is creating the obstacles? My friend Jenny knows how it feels to have everything look right on the outside, yet there's still some mysterious internal force causing turmoil.

> "I look pretty great on paper. No broken home; my parents have been married for almost 48 years. No poverty. No excessive wealth either, but we were never lacking and are certainly comfortable."

Jenny's been happily married for eighteen years, has two healthy daughters, and has never struggled to find gainful employment. She currently works as a program consultant for a nutrition company, and has a wealth of knowledge on how to improve and maintain good physical health.

If you meet Jenny, she's calm and confident, certainly engaging. This is a woman who shows up at public events by herself and mingles with ease. She had the guts to try roller derby at age forty and stuck with it, in spite of a tough learning curve and several injuries. Even when you get close to her, she still gives off the impression that she has everything under control.

In total transparency, I didn't consider Jenny as a potential participant in *Women Ready to Rise* until a year into this project. Although I knew her life couldn't possibly be perfect, she appeared to have a pretty enviable one.

It wasn't until her daughter came forward with a shocking confession of self-harm that I discovered Jenny was secretly at war with herself.

"There's always been this pervasive feeling of not fitting in. Which is really fucking hard to explain to someone when I have all the 'right' boxes checked off, but still don't feel good enough. But I'm not supposed to talk about that. If I dare say anything, I'm met with a wall of people spouting platitudes about how nice I have it, how I'm OK, how great my husband and kids are, etc. It's like being ostracized from the transformational community because it's 'just' this feeling of not being good enough. I'm not broken enough, which of course is ridiculous!"

I unknowingly contributed to her feeling of not fitting in, partially due to this story. Jenny never expressed those feelings to me prior to asking for her involvement; I suspect she was used to keeping everything bottled up inside. It is something she's conscientiously working on changing. She knew how important it was for her daughter to open up and talk about her feelings, and now Jenny shares her emotions more freely with her close friends. She finally opened up about how she felt when I asked her why she thought I wanted her in this book.

"I felt like I wasn't fucked up or tragic enough to be in your book, which was somewhat of a relief. Nobody *wants* to be fucked up or experience tragedy, and in that respect I have been fortunate. I'd love to be a voice for those just like me, who are not entirely OK—but others only see all of the reasons why they should be."

I didn't pick any "fucked-up" people for this book, and that's actually why Jenny does fit in. *Women Ready to Rise* is full of stories about finding purpose in our pain. I was inspired to ask Jenny when she, as well as her brave daughter, decided to talk about their mental health issues publicly.

Due to the stupid stigma surrounding any mental health disorder, admitting it out loud is a sincerely difficult thing to do. Her thirteen-year-old daughter decided to share her personal story as part of a campaign to raise funds for mental health programs. Jenny put her full support behind the endeavor.

> "My 13-year-old daughter went into her annual doctor's appointment and came out the other side with a confession of self-harm and not feeling safe enough to go home, as she feared she might hurt herself further. That night in the emergency department, as she went through triage, I heard things I had never known about my baby. I learned how she'd been hurting herself in an attempt to feel something, anything, other than a consuming darkness.
>
> "I learned she'd been hearing voices and seeing things that are not there. While my daughter was in with the social worker, I sat alone in a chair, inwardly freaking out. I was texting my husband and my coach. How was I going to keep it together for her when I wasn't sure I could keep it together for myself? If I hadn't been working on resources for myself the last few months, I think I would have shattered into even more pieces."

This is why we need to talk about it. Having access to meaningful resources can literally be the difference between life and death. Jenny knows how terrified she felt when her daughter admitted to harming herself and hearing voices. That would undeniably be frightening for any parent. The alarming reality of how the situation could have unfolded did not escape her. She recognized that her own feelings of inadequacy and the anxiety that she was squashing down on the inside were beginning to manifest in her daughters.

In that terrifying wake-up call, Jenny realized that she could no longer hide in the dark, pretending everything was fine. She had to turn on a light and raise awareness, to encourage other parents to initiate discussions with their children.

Jenny's vulnerability in an effort to inspire others is what makes her a woman ready to rise.

"Anxiety and darkness can be battled with love. Unconditional, brilliant, beautiful love. The pure love I felt the moment I held my little girl in my arms and became a mom. The vulnerable love born from the reality that I cannot protect her from everything. She will face her own demons, but she doesn't have to face them alone. Neither do I."

Her daughter was raised in a home where she felt comfortable talking about her mental health, thankfully. As her new teenager and soon-to-be teenager venture into a drastically changing world, it's critical that they feel comfortable talking about the important issues affecting their lives.

Since receiving Jenny's answers for this story, she's had the usual share of adulting-sucks bullshit and modern-day parental stress, coupled with feelings of loneliness or anxiety. I know when she's going through most of it now, because she feels comfortable talking about it in a safe community of friends who care about her. We have a group chat where we share our daily WTFs and OMGs, encouraging whoever needs it the most.

Jenny still struggles with anxiety, but is working on ways to make it more manageable. She takes time to meditate and reflect on what's happening in her life. She recognizes when it feels like her world is spinning out of control, and can ask for help when it's needed. Slowly but surely, she's becoming more comfortable expressing the chaos in her mind.

A lack of trauma doesn't mean Jenny's had an easy life, and there were experiences from her younger years that were lingering inside. She was bullied as a teen, ostracized by the unfortunate cattiness that plagues young women. That often manifests into a feeling of never fitting in later in life.

Jenny had to uproot her family and move to a city where she knew no one. Shortly after moving away from her family and friends, her brother's fiancé, who was also her friend, lost a brief battle with cancer at age 24. Those experiences triggered her anxiety, and then taught her ways to cope with it. Now Jenny is doing her best to maintain open communication with her kids about their mental health, while being honest with herself about how she's feeling.

Unlike a broken bone or a cancer diagnosis, mental health issues are not as obvious or taken as seriously. Quite often, even the person suffering with the illness is unaware that there is a legitimate problem. We're taught to trust our own minds and when the mind is the one playing games, it becomes hard to trust our own thoughts.

Not everyone's struggles are obvious to an outside observer, but that doesn't make them any less real or challenging. In some cases, it's so much harder because no one else can see your pain. Of course, that leads to hiding or ignoring it, which only makes it worse.

Mental health is just as fragile and critical to our survival as physical health. We should feel comfortable discussing it the same way we talk about diabetes or a broken bone. Jenny and her daughter's honesty in a quest to help others are proof she's so strong that she can even rise above her own mind.

The subject matter of my first book has connected me with countless survivors from all over the world. Although I haven't met most of them in person, our mutual advocacy and passion for change forges an instant bond. One of the most open and honest mental health advocates I've met along my journey is Jody. When I asked her why she thought I felt she was right for this book, she knew the reason.

"I hope you chose me because despite what I deal with on a daily basis, I advocate and encourage as much as I can. I am raw and open with my feelings, so others know they are not alone in their thoughts and emotions."

We connected on Twitter, where Jody pours her heart into every Tweet. Living your personal struggles out loud takes more courage than people realize. In most cases, her passionate tweets exposing her mental health struggles and suicidal thoughts are met with appreciation and/or concern. In some instances, she is attacked for sharing her feelings, or accused of doing it for attention. Online bullying can be brutal, but she doesn't let it get to her. Jody's survived much worse.

"My abuse began when I was just six months old, and continued until I was fourteen. I was not abused by a family member, but instead by numerous predators ranging from fourteen to fifty years old, including a soccer coach. I was gang raped at a party when I was sixteen, by a bunch of kids from a neighboring school. They drugged my drink, and I'm only able to remember parts of it. Since there were so many abusers, it took me a great number of years to truly understand that it was not my fault. I thought that I must have been doing or saying something that attracted these types of people repeatedly.

"It wasn't until a few years ago that I learned that predators sense the vulnerability in a child, like me; I became easy prey. At the same time, there was domestic violence in my home, and I spent much of my time there trying to console and listen to my mom. I protected her in any way possible, which I learned at a later age is an impossible task for a child, and a position I should not have been placed in at all."

Being born with alcohol in her bloodstream, raised in an unstable home, and forced to grow up faster than she should have laid a rocky foundation for Jody's future. Her fragile world was further shattered by the loss of her mom when she was only nineteen. Her mom was diagnosed with cancer when Jody was thirteen years old, and it was a long six years of surgeries, remissions, chemotherapy, radiation, and hospitals before her mother finally lost her battle with cancer.

"The hardest part for me, aside from watching her suffer for so long, was having no control whatsoever. I may not have always helped, but I tried my best to protect my mom from the abuse. I tried my best to be her friend and confidante, but I was simply too young. With the cancer, all I could do was watch her slowly die. To this day, my mind has separated my life into two parts: before my mom died, and after."

I would guess my friends Kim and Lisa from the earlier chapters feel the same way. I can see how our minds separate our lives into pre and post when we go through something traumatic, especially the loss of a loved one. I'm sure many women reading these raw confessions will relate to the need to divide our lives into more manageable segments. We do whatever we need to do in order to survive.

Jody was victimized her entire upbringing, permanently scarring her mental well-being. As a result of the post traumatic stress, from those experiences in her developmental years and the immense heartbreak she has faced since, Jody fights every day to stay alive. Today, she miraculously manages to resist chronic suicidal ideations that haunt her mind, but it wasn't always possible. She was only eight years old when she made her first attempt, and still battles these internal demons.

"My first attempt at age eight was written off as 'childhood misadventure,' and never spoken of again. I slit my wrists when I was thirteen, overdosed at sixteen, and then failed hanging myself in my early thirties. There were a few more overdoses at home, and my last failed attempt was in 2000. I was never hospitalized, not once, for more than a few hours.

"At the lowest points in my life, I have lost all sense of direction and hope. The darkness in my mind takes over everything. Emotions, conversations, your sense of self, are all swallowed whole by a vast dark hole. I feel completely alone, and often feel like there is no point to this life. Having no kids or family that cares makes it a lot easier to want to give up, since your death will have no effect on them anyway.

"I feel like an emotional burden on the few people I have in my life. I feel like no matter what medication or treatments I try, I will never be well enough to function 'normally' in this world, and that makes facing each day a challenge. It often feels like you cannot believe the good things people may say about you; those words are easily swallowed by the darkness."

I most certainly believe the good things people say about Jody. I follow online as she lifts up others, assuring them that there is always hope, no matter how bleak her own life might feel in the moment. I asked Jody to share her story because of the difficult past she's had to conquer, but also because her battle is ongoing. The darkness still tries to creep into her mind; she has to conscientiously search for enough light to see the road ahead, and keep herself moving forward. Jody is a woman ready to rise because she continues to fight to stay alive every day, in spite of an overwhelming feeling of wanting to die.

"It wasn't until my breakdown a few years ago that I actually started to take care of my mental health. Prior to that, I ignored it and did pretty much anything to avoid dealing with the thoughts consuming my mind. I have often been asked what has kept me going for so long, and I really have no answer—aside from the fact that I have been on both ends of suicide, and I really don't want to hurt anyone.

"I think that is a common theme among people with these ideations. I joined Twitter several years ago, and that is where I became involved with SickNotWeak, a mental health charity foundation. I became very close friends with Michael Landsberg, who has been my greatest support. I truly credit him with helping to keep me alive during the crisis moments. The Twitter mental health community itself is an incredible space to give and receive support, with no judgment. Now I offer inexpensive online support sessions, so people can have at least some support while waiting for therapy, or for those who simply cannot afford therapy."

Twitter and the mental health community have been a huge part of Jody's healing process, as well as giving her a platform for her writing and a voice for her fight for better mental healthcare. She took the support she received from Michael Landsberg and is regifting it to those she encounters. Using her experiences to encourage others who are struggling with similar thoughts has given Jody a purpose for her pain.

"I am proud of my writing, and one article in particular: 'I Want You to Want to Live.' I submitted it to themighty.com, and it was one of my first articles they published. Since then, it has had more hits than any article on the site. It is basically a letter to those in crisis, from someone who lives mostly in crisis. I know from experience that we often do not want to hear some of the scripted conversation of a crisis line, so I decided to write down some things that I know I would want to hear in my moments of life and death, in hopes that maybe it would reach someone in their time of need.

"I have received well over 1,000 direct messages from people saying thank you or reaching out for help. I have responded to each and every one, and helped the best I can. I am proud of the size of audience that my article has reached, that it has been published by numerous other publications, and even translated into a few different languages. I feel humbled to be able to indirectly help someone in their time of need."

Jody's outpouring of emotion is inspiring strength in others. That's the core purpose behind this entire story. When we share our hardships and methods for coping, we give hope to those who are dealing with the same kind of pain.

"When I am suicidal and have no hope, I hold on for one important reason: so I don't hurt the few people who care about me. I have lived with daily suicidal thoughts for forty years, and have convinced myself that it is better that I continue to suffer rather than inflict pain on others by taking my life.

"Right now, I am staying alive because my friend is dying of bone cancer. I know she needs my love and support. If I hurt myself, she would be devastated. I tell people to hold on for whatever they can, be it something as simple as your pet needs to be fed or walked tomorrow. Hold on to what you can, day by day, hour by hour, minute by minute. Someone needs you, whether you realize it or not."

I know it's difficult for Jody to absorb compliments, but the life-saving work she is doing is noticed and appreciated. She is a thriving survivor, and I'm grateful that she fights to keep living every single day. I hope her story gives you the strength to keep going on the days when it feels like you simply can't go on.

ABUSE ALWAYS GETS WORSE

I met Renee through my Facebook group, and there was an immediate connection resonating between us. We had several hardships in common, as we both watched while our mothers were poorly treated by men; we grew up thinking that anger and insults were a normal part of life. The lack of genuine love in Renee's developmental years resulted in tragically low self-esteem that misguided her throughout all of her romantic relationships. Boy, can I relate to that.

> "I felt very unloved as a child and had low self-esteem. My dad cheated on my mom relentlessly, even parading those women in front of me and my siblings. I grew up believing his example was the way I deserved to be treated by men. I held on to those daddy issues well into adulthood.
>
> "I dated some truly nice, decent men, but would break things off with them when they got too close. I was convinced that they would break up with me once they figured out that I wasn't good enough for them."

The first twenty years of life sets the foundation and expectations that we carry with us through the rest of our lives. We can learn ways to succeed in spite of negative baggage, and reach a place where it no longer dominates our train of thought, but it never fully disappears. I'm an intelligent, successful, kind, popular, attractive, happily married author who has finished marathons: super impressive on paper. My self-esteem is still unstable, and quite often I need to remind myself that I'm worthy. Renee understands.

Children are continuously growing physically, but mentally and emotionally as well. The events we face at that age create our perception of reality. Renee's childhood taught her that she couldn't count on her parents, love was conditional, and violent fits were just an expected aspect of being alive.

> "My older brother was diagnosed as being paranoid schizophrenic with bipolar disorder. He drank to stop the voices, but the drinking made him mean with a very volatile temper. My younger sister and I literally had to barricade ourselves in our bedroom at night. Physical family violence was a constant companion growing up in our house. We couldn't have friends over, because you never knew what he might do. I believe that one of the reasons my father abandoned us is that he didn't know how to deal with my brother."

Growing up in a toxic home and being abandoned or verbally abused by your father often leads to falling for manipulative men, because you're craving acceptance and approval. There are cases where it inspires the child in a positive way to avoid making similar mistakes. Unfortunately, that usually only happens when the parent being abused is open and honest about their regrets and hardships; most victims are too afraid to say anything, to anyone.

I saw abusive behavior as a child and found myself in an abusive relationship; the pattern repeats itself until it's acknowledged. It's easy for women like Renee and me to ignore subtle signs of trouble, because so many of the relationships we saw growing up were not healthy examples of love. Renee married a man she thought would save her from a toxic family environment. Then she discovered he was both a rageaholic and an alcoholic.

> "I didn't see the rage until after we were married with our first child. His temper terrified me, but I was more afraid of being

alone. My daughter was three when my son was born nine-and-a-half weeks early, at *3 pounds four ounces* in 1989."

Being a parent of two young children, especially when one is premature, is already a significant amount of stress for a person to handle. The thought of handling the additional demands as a single parent is legitimately frightening. It's not surprising that she was afraid to be alone.

Renee's son initially spent two months in the neonatal intensive care unit (NICU). He was discharged, then in and out of the hospital for the next two months. He suddenly became gravely ill with a respiratory infection and was airlifted to a hospital two hours away, where they would spend the next two years fighting for her son's life.

"We were constantly required to make life or death decisions on his behalf. Our marriage began to crack from the pressure. I refused to give up on anything and thought I was Superwoman. I tried to fix everybody except myself."

Having a child with severe, chronic medical issues sent Renee's life down a completely different path than the one she had previously laid out for herself. Prior to experiencing the extra challenges motherhood would bring for her, her focus was on ensuring she stayed on track. Renee worked full time while she was pregnant, as well as taking courses at night towards her associate degree. She was ready to balance family and her future career aspirations.

Just like Kimberly earlier in the book, after her son was born, Elijah became her first priority. Her life was consumed with keeping him alive, and that meant she had to stop taking the classes. She was focused on her baby boy, while her husband only seemed interested in taking care of his own needs.

"I hit rock bottom when I caught my husband cheating. I was devastated. Here I was, putting my all into our marriage, and he just shit all over it. I started therapy again. I cried a lot. I was terrified of having to raise my son alone. I begged him not to leave me, and he used it as leverage.

"I made a promise to myself that I would never allow him to get close enough to me to hurt me like that again. I opened a separate savings account and named it Mad Money. Every time he made me mad, I'd make a deposit. I didn't have a support network at the time, which made me feel even more alone. I began to build my support network and planned an escape. He continued to use his rage to shut me down."

How long did it take Renee to save up enough in her Mad Money account to leave?

I am about to share something that may shock some readers, considering the other stories you've read so far, but Renee's story doesn't have a happy ending yet. It will get there, though; I believe she can be both on the rise and still restrained.

In spite of still being in the heart of her tragedy, Renee's story is more powerful than you first might realize. No, she hasn't yet left a man who has repeatedly broken her heart and her spirit, as well as stripped her of her confidence. That's unfortunate; however, she recognizes that change is mandatory, and is working on ending her marriage. She's laying a new foundation so that she can rebuild a better life for her and her son.

Until you are actually in a person's specific situation, please don't judge. Admitting your relationship is toxic is a huge step forward, and why I see a woman ready to rise in Renee. Leaving an abusive marriage is a difficult, draining endeavor that takes time, even when we know it's the right thing to do. It doesn't happen instantly.

"I began to build my support network. I planned, and he continued to use his rage to shut me down. But I continued to reach out to people, because I knew that I couldn't do it alone. I continued to plan my escape. I continued to work on my self-esteem issues. I grew stronger and more confident. I got tired of his lies, and finally confronted him one day. He yelled at me and *I yelled back*, no longer afraid.

"He tried to put the blame on me, but I flipped the script on him this time. It threw him off balance, and he stormed out of the house. I felt empowered, and I let him go. He came back the next day and the next one after that, saying that he was looking for an apartment. I only said, 'Uh, huh,' and let him go.

"On day three, he asked if he could stay. I said, 'It's your house too.' He came back. Nothing has changed, except that now I have a solid plan in place for my son. The final confrontation is coming any day now. I know and deeply understand in my soul that I don't need him, and *I am enough*. I am tired, and not willing to put up with his shit anymore. I just need to make sure that my support network for my son is solid before I make my move."

Realizing you deserve better is the first step, but it takes constant reassurance to continue believing it when you live with someone who tears down your self-esteem. Creating a plan of action is the next step, and ensuring your own safety and sanity through the process is essential. Of course, when children are involved—especially when the child requires extensive medical care—it becomes much harder to take that necessary leap of faith.

"My life is literally in flux right now. We received a call from my son's neurologist last night, and he's referring my son to an oncologist because of something discovered in his bloodwork yesterday. I feel devastated, but I'm trying to stay positive."

Renee is trying, and she will rise. I have faith in her. I couldn't admit to anything my ex was doing when we were still together. I was too ashamed, and assumed everyone would think I was a fool. It wasn't until years later that I realized it wasn't my fault, and those who loved me would have been there to support me throughout those soul-crushing moments, had I been honest about what was going on. By sharing her experiences in this book, even using an alias, Renee is taking a huge leap forward.

"I've just confronted my husband for what will be the last time. His lies are suffocating me, and this is *it*. I've been seeing a therapist since February to sort through my issues. I'd moved my son out of our home last November, in with a 'friend' of mine, so that I could move forward with my plan to leave. This was a huge step for me; the last time I moved him into a group home several years ago, it turned out to be a nightmare.

"I expected he'd be well cared for this time, since it was someone I knew. However, she wasn't taking care of his personal hygiene in an acceptable manner, and was using his personal supplies for herself. I'd noticed that he'd lost five pounds in May, and that was the last straw.

"My therapist helped me see that this person is a narcissist, just like my husband. I've been surrounded by them all my life! The difference now is that I can see them for what they are and have much better skills in dealing with them, and not allowing new ones into my life.

"I moved my son back home in June out of necessity and with a heavy heart. I'm his legal guardian as well as his mother, so I have a legal as well as moral obligation to ensure his health and well being. I am scared things will go back to the way they were. What I realized is that they will only go back that way if I *allow* them to, and I'm not about to let that happen! I have taken back my power, and I realize that I have more power than I ever knew.

"I'm still with the husband, and he's once again the primary caregiver of our son—for now. He no longer rages at me, as he's figured out that it doesn't work on me anymore, and I'm not afraid of him. He never thought I'd move our son out and begin to move on with my life. That was eye opening for him.

"I'm in the process of looking for someone trustworthy to provide care for my son, but it won't be easy. I don't have any family near me, so it's even more difficult. My son is nonverbal and can't tell me if he's being mistreated. I still plan on leaving, I just have to rearrange the timing.

"I recently came across this quote from Zig Ziglar: 'When obstacles arise, you change your direction to reach your goal; you do not change your decision to get there.' This fits my situation perfectly. It will take longer than I expected, but I won't be deterred. I deserve to be happy in my second act, and I'm refusing to settle for anything less."

Renee knows she deserves better, and she will get there when the time is right. If her experiences ring a little too true with you, please speak up. Message me online, tell someone you trust, or contact a professional therapist. Talking about abuse will help undo the damage and alleviate the feeling of shame or blame, so you can rise too.

My next risen woman is another fellow domestic abuse survivor whom I connected with online after publishing my first book, *Dark Confessions of an Extraordinary, Ordinary Woman*. We've never met in person, but I feel confident stating JJ will be a friend for life.

"Jenn and I connected through social media when her first book came out. When you're a survivor, newly out of an abusive relationship and/or trauma, you look anywhere and everywhere for someone like you. I wanted to know that I wasn't the crazy one: that my mood swings, fits of crying, triggers, and fears were a normal reaction to a horrific situation.

"Jenn's story connected with my own on so many levels. Since then, both of us have moved on to find fulfilling and healthy relationships. We have worked hard to rebuild our lives, but we have remained in touch and have continued to support one another online."

It is alarming how many domestic violence survivors I've met online since my first book was released; way too common of an experience. JJ has worked hard to rebound from her trauma, and is creating a fulfilling life. She seeks out support and recognizes triggers, which is not easy for someone who has been convinced she's unworthy. She understands when to fight and when to walk away to preserve her own peace of mind. JJ has gone through more than her share of tough days, and is now focused on creating a happy life for herself and her family.

"From the time I was 16 until I was almost 40 years old, I was in a relationship with—and eventually married—a narcissist with untreated bipolar disorder. I had no idea he'd been diagnosed with this when I met him, and I don't know if I'd even have cared, because I wanted to rescue him from his awful childhood. For years, he stole from me and my family. He raped me when he was addicted to drugs (and never remembered because he was so high), and abused my beloved pets. He called me a 'cheap Jew' and belittled my faith (he's also Jewish, interestingly enough).

"My ex insulted me so much that I stopped going to synagogue. We stopped vacationing with my family, who were always a big part of my life. And then he pushed me to stop working. He'd convinced me I was a bad mother for working twenty hours a week, fifteen minutes from home, at a job I adored and felt good about. People suspected something was wrong, but I never admitted to anything. I was always 'fine.'"

If you've never been in a relationship with a manipulative narcissist, it's hard to understand why so many women get trapped in relationships that we know are not healthy. Men like JJ's ex will build trust first, making you feel special, and then slowly strip away your self-esteem. It's so cleverly done that most women have no idea what's going on until it's too late.

"I felt ashamed. I was embarrassed that an educated person like me—someone who'd been the top student in her major, graduated college and graduate school with honors, someone who'd worked for world-class hospitals, with the top physicians in her field—could have been snowed the way I was by him.

"My mind still runs wild to this day, full of thoughts about how I could have known better and what I should have done. I have two degrees in psychology, for Chrissakes! I was so deeply in denial, I didn't know if the sky was really blue. If it weren't for a group of psychiatrists I worked for, I may have never realized the horror I was living with."

My educational background is not as impressive as JJ's, but I'm pretty damn smart too. So is Renee, from earlier in this chapter. We would all love to assume we are too wise to be played for a fool, but it can happen to anyone. Narcissists fuck with your mind to the extent you can no longer trust your own thoughts.

Although she'd tried leaving once before and went back, JJ's final straw was this: a few days after bringing home a dog for her daughter, her ex threatened to take it to the pound. Threatening a defenseless animal or child is quite often what it takes for women to leave. Women always seem more concerned about how the abuse is affecting everyone else, rather than the trauma it is causing them.

"That night, as I watched him sleep, my rage and hatred finally bubbled to the surface. The over twenty years of insults, theft, erratic spending, mood swings, coercive and outward control, threats that his hands were 'getting hot,' drug abuse, rape, lies, and isolation finally crashed together and swarmed my brain. In that moment, I realized that I needed to make a plan to leave. I wished he was dead."

It's OK to wish he was dead, and really important to leave before you actually do it. I fantasized about my ex dying; it was never by my hand, but it was always something sudden and tragic. If you ever think that you'd prefer the person you're with to be dead, it's time to end it.

"I didn't tell anyone what was going on, due to the shame I felt about living with this monstrosity for so long. I called my old boss at the hospital, asked if I could volunteer until our daughter started kindergarten full time, when I could start working. That was two years away, but I didn't tell him about my plan to leave my marriage and that I needed a job desperately to help me obtain and maintain my independence. He gladly took me back, and together we developed a job that would give me the freedom to be a single parent, and get back the career I loved so much.

"I didn't tell my ex-husband. Secretly, I asked my mother-in-law to watch my daughter while I volunteered three half-days a week. She knew that if he found out, he'd be extremely angry. At the time, she kept my secret. She didn't know about my plan to leave him. She thought her son walked on water and could do no wrong.

"My point in spilling all of these details about my plan is to tell every reader that I made a huge mistake. *I didn't tell anyone about my plan to leave an abusive relationship.* That is the first rule of leaving a toxic relationship, for obvious safety reasons, and in order to maximize the chances of becoming independent and not going back."

You can't do it alone, and people will help. When someone reaches out to me who is still stuck in an abusive relationship, the first thing I do is encourage them to tell someone they love or trust as much as you can. Tell your parents, a sibling, a professional therapist, or a police officer; it can be anyone, as long as someone is there to help you through it.

JJ didn't tell anyone how bad things were and when her ex manipulated her into participating in something she didn't know was illegal, there was no one who could back up her story that she wasn't his equal partner in crime. Although she has absolutely no reason to feel shame, JJ didn't discuss the hardest experience she went through with her ex in her official interview answers.

However, she touched on being in jail briefly in one answer, and it was part of a necessary warning to women. I felt it was essential to include her quote, which is a little later in her story. I sent a brief email inquiring if she was willing to discuss the circumstances that led to such a shocking situation for this intelligent, successful woman. Her response sums up the seeds of doubt, insecurities, and the massive mindfuck caused by narcissistic men.

"Ugh... It's a part of my life that doesn't even feel like it was me. I guess I try to forget it and pretend it didn't happen. I went to jail instead of risking a trial and possibly getting sentenced to worse than four months away from my daughter. The case was very political, and the judge had significant pressure from my ex's former employer to punish both of us. He masterminded the whole thing, and manipulated me into thinking they knew. He convinced me that everything was OK with what he was doing.

"General perception in the courts is that as a spouse, you're educated and you should know better. But when you are mentally and emotionally beaten down for two decades, you can't make a decision without asking if it's OK. You're told stories and gaslighted by your own spouse whom you desperately don't want to see as a monster. There's no way to know better. At that point, it's about surviving, every day, with your sanity as intact as it can be.

"This really has to change within the court system as a whole. Judges are sorely undereducated about the literal brain changes that happen when one lives this way. I still kick myself all the time for believing him, because in the back of my mind I knew something was very wrong. I didn't know how to stop it, or even begin to address it."

Narcissists are cunning liars. It's undetectable. The confidence with which they spin a tale makes even the most bizarre scenario sound conceivable. This happened quite a few years ago, and JJ is still punishing herself for his mistakes. He still rents space in her head, though she kicks the thought of him out anytime he tries to creep in. Abuse by the person who is supposed to love you the most has a lifelong, lasting impact. To this day, she still second-guesses herself at work and at home when it comes to making even simple decisions.

"I didn't know at that point—or maybe I didn't admit it to myself—that I had been a victim of domestic violence. The cultural view of DV is that of regular beatings, affairs, drinking, drugs, fire setting, child abuse, kidnapping, and all sorts of overt, violent behavior. In truth, the abuse I endured is much more common than that noted above. Plus, it occurred in cycles as opposed to the media-portrayed norm of abuse happening as a constant. This, in general, is not the case."

By the grace of God, JJ was able to see how dangerous her situation was, and she got out before it was too late. Many women are not as lucky, and of course, there's Renee who's still trying to safely leave. That knowledge is what gave JJ the courage to share intimate details of what she went through, and why she is passing it on to you.

"A lot of people say they found God in jail or in prison; now I understand why. For me, I see that so many things happened for a reason. When we were arrested, ten weapons were found in our house. What would have happened if he'd snapped?"

The most dangerous time for a victim of abuse is when she attempts to leave. This is why JJ stresses having a plan and telling someone. There are resources everywhere. If you can't find one, message me on social media and I'll help connect you with services in your area. Your life matters. People will help.

"By good luck, I had a great attorney, a therapist who had significant experience with trauma victims, and parents and family who stood by me and did whatever they could to keep me positive. I was blessed, and even though I'd been isolated for so long, those who truly cared for me and believed in me stepped up and were there. A friend and former colleague I hadn't seen in years wrote to me regularly. I became thankful for the small things, and those things that really mattered. I was given these gifts when I hit my lowest point.

"You know what I just realized and it's absolutely mind-blowing! I think this is something to point out, because I had to get that low to get out. Getting arrested is what got me out of my marriage. The lowest point in my life was also one of the best things that could have happened to me, because it forced me to blow my cover and to take a good, hard look at what had happened to my life and that of our daughter. He literally placed me and his four-year old daughter in harm's way, so we could have clothes, sports cars, watches, jewelry and anything else you could possibly think of materially. It was all an illusion, and it ruined all of our lives. I'm still so, so angry about it."

Pow! That is powerful. Her life didn't magically fix itself. JJ had to rebuild her career while advocating for herself through social services until she could support her and her daughter. She reached out online to other survivors, building herself an emotional support network. She attended therapy at a local shelter, and eventually started dating again. There is love after abuse, if you're brave enough to put yourself back out there. Listen to how smitten JJ is with her new love.

"His love for nature, animals, and children touched me. His relationship with his parents and commitment to them were endearing. Fast forward to several years later; we recently celebrated our fourth wedding anniversary. Even though we don't have a lot materially, I am happier than I ever was with my ex. He loves and treats my daughter as his own, and is more of a father to her than my ex ever was or ever could be.

"He has literally picked me up off the floor when I couldn't do it myself, wrestled knives away from me when I was in the throes of self-injury and PTSD episodes, and loved me for *me*, even with all of my complications and faults. He helped me realize that I *am* worthy, and there *is* someone out there who will love and respect me for me. We've both been to therapy, alone and together (he's also a survivor of a narcissist), and has patiently worked with me on all of my challenges."

JJ is happily married, raising a well-rounded, well-cared for daughter, and has a career that makes her proud. She's helping others, and knows that she also deserves help. She's worthy, and a shining example that if a man knocks you down, trust that you have the power to stand back up.

STOLEN INNOCENCE

Manipulation and abuse can cause so much more damage when it's directed at a child. There is no crime greater than abusing a child, especially sexual abuse. It's easy to equate it to murder, due to the permanent destruction it causes.

Every child is born innocent and deserves to have a real chance at a good life. The two lovely ladies in this chapter are exceptionally inspiring. I just wish they would have had the chance to become the women they are now without first having to overcome such severe trauma.

Sexual abuse is viewed as being a taboo subject that's almost never discussed. The thought of it happening to a child is horrifically gut wrenching to imagine. As a vocal survivor of domestic abuse, numerous women have reached out to me over the past five years with brutal stories of sexual abuse. I usually only skim through the details, because it's too enraging and disturbing to read the heartbreaking violations of a woman's body. For Steph's story, I had to dive in deep and fight back the anger.

I hope you will too. As hard as it is to read what she endured at such a young age, there is something extraordinarily inspiring about how Steph handled the entire ordeal. It's also unbelievably impressive how she found a way to move forward and is now living this happy, empowering life.

"I went through a tragedy starting at a very young age that lasted over a decade of my life. Since I have overcome it and I am now living my best life possible, I want to help and inspire others. From this tragedy, I want women in the same boat to know there is a light on the other side of that tunnel. I had every odd against me and I rose above it all."

Steph was a sex slave to her uncle, starting sometime around age three or four. Of course, at that age, she was too young to be aware of the damage her uncle was causing, or that he was even doing something wrong. He showered her with attention and affection, bought her gifts, and convinced her that she was his special girl.

***Please be aware that I'm about to share the details of what Steph experienced for anyone who finds this too triggering.

I feel that describing Steph's sexual abuse is necessary, despite how much it makes my stomach turn. I understand that no one wants to hear how she was groomed, or the extent of his predatory behavior. However, awareness is the only way to recognize the signs and break through the stigma. This gives others the courage to speak up.

Child predators are master manipulators. It's a slow, methodical game plan. Her uncle began sexually abusing her by wanting her to sleep naked next to him. That led to fondling, and then slowly sticking himself inside her until he could fit his entire penis in at age six.

"Parents always told me it's OK if family sees you naked, but not strangers. He was family, and I didn't know any better. He started taking me for sleepovers at his house, and he would make me sleep naked in his bed, next to him naked. He said I couldn't tell anyone; the gifts and special attention came with our secret. I didn't want to sleep over, but I would because I got new Barbies and money if I did.

"This continued throughout my childhood. What started as touching, caressing, fondling, turned into rape. He was never mean or malicious about it. I wasn't held down or restrained. If I did give him a hard time, he would say, 'When people love each other, this is what they do for each other.'

"He was my family, and I was told I had to love my family. He used to tell me that as soon as I was old enough, I would be having his children and we'd get married. I was brainwashed, but I truly believed all of this for the longest time. Even now I believe he truly loved me, and if I never told anyone that I'd still be trapped with him.

"He was always at my house; he'd offer to babysit me and my brothers, drive us to school, or bring me back to his house for lunch. I had to spend every weekend at his place, and during the summer, sometimes more. He had everyone fooled."

Abusers, rapists, murders, the most dangerous people in this world are always people you would never expect. 'The greatest trick the devil ever pulled was convincing the world he didn't exist.' It takes a sociopath to violate or physically harm another human being. Anyone capable of what Steph is about to describe is also skilled at hiding any signs of their evil.

"I have one vivid memory of when I realized what was happening was not really normal, or I started questioning what he was doing. This was around age nine. I was sitting on the edge of the bed; he was standing in front of me, and he had his penis out and making me hold it. He said put it in your mouth like it's a lollipop and suck it.

"I remember crying saying I didn't want to and begging him to not make me. He said, 'I kiss you and lick you, now you must do it to me.' He grabbed his penis and gently put it in my mouth. At nine years old, I performed oral sex.

"He would make me watch porn with him and told me I had to learn to do what the girls were doing. By age ten, he was also having anal sex with me. He never used protection, even when I started getting my periods. He knew pregnancy could be a risk. He was happy when I started periods, meaning I was becoming more woman and closer to our 'exclusive life together,' as he described it.

"I knew the drill: get to his house, go inside, and take my clothes off. I'd sit on the bed and wait for him. He started using toys on me. Honestly when it comes to sex, you name it, I had done it with him. His little sex slave, that I was.

"I tried everything to get him to stop. I wouldn't shower, thinking maybe if I stank, he wouldn't want me. I tried not to wear any clothing that would be considered cute or make me look appealing. I would fight with my mom not to go to his place. He always used to tell me guys don't like fat girls. So I gained weight on purpose, in the hope he wouldn't like me anymore.

"I became very cold and distant toward everyone in my life. I dropped out of gymnastics. I wanted to go to the Olympics, but I gave it up. I stopped karate, all my extracurriculars that I enjoyed and loved. By this point, I didn't love myself. I didn't love him. I envied my friends for no reason. I hated everything. But I had one thing that understood me. That was Tommy; Tommy was my safeguard, a little stuffed kitty cat I got when I was small. Tommy went everywhere with me."

This continued for ten years. Due to the amount of time the two families spent together, no one knew what was going on. This disgusting abuse consumed her childhood, and yet it was not strong enough to destroy Steph. At an age when I was causing mayhem and running from the cops, Steph had the smarts and strength to go to the police.

"Finally, in the summer after grade 8, I told the cops. I was at his house, and after he sexually abused me, I told him I was going outside to call a friend who lived close by, to see if they could hang out. I called 911. I remember the police telling me not to go back into the house, to meet them at McDonald's instead. I went back inside to grab my favorite stuffed toy, Tommy, and told my uncle I was going to the store."

She was so young and broken down, but still had the courage to take matters into her own hands. Steph had reached a breaking point where she knew that she'd had enough, mustered the strength to vocalize what he was doing to her, and was finally able to break free from the abuse.

"Earlier in the day, my friend's mom said I looked broken and upset. Maybe that's why I called the police. Maybe I was ready? Longest night ever! I met the cops at McDonald's, who took me to the hospital. I had to hand over all of my clothing, nail clippings and hair samples were taken, photos of marks, swabs, bloodwork, etc. I remember lots of doctors and nurses. Everyone was being so nice, and saying that it's not my fault. Some even cried when they heard everything. I don't think anyone was prepared to hear it had been going on for ten years.

"When my parents showed up, that's when I realized what he had been doing to me was wrong. It was when I saw my parents that I suddenly felt dirty and ashamed, and wished I never told anyone. I had to talk to the police, Children's Aid Society, and a lady from the sexual assault crisis center. I don't know how many times I told my story that night."

She was not even in high school, yet she had to openly discuss so much trauma with so many people. I am grateful that she had the courage to discuss it once again, with all of us. It's important to shed light on abuse and show how easily it can happen to anyone. As it is *never* the victim's fault; there is no reason to hide what happened in shame.

A sexual assault survivor's strength often appears surreal to those who haven't suffered through the same. Many survivors are questioned or called out as fake, because their calm and precise recollection of events doesn't jive with how most would assume a victim would behave. On the other hand, some sexual abuse survivors are erratic, emotional, and inconsistent when they attempt to retell what they experienced. Some block it out; others have the trauma looping through their mind so often that it no longer makes them shudder.

Steph vividly remembers the days following her freeing herself from the abuse, and how what he did to her can never be undone.

"We went to McDonald's drive-thru to pick me up dinner, at 4 a.m. I went home, straight to bed. I woke up a few hours later to both of my brothers standing in my room, looking at me. They looked at me like I was broken/damaged.

"I got up, and continued on with my life. Everyone came over: all my family, all my friends. I guess my parents had been up all night calling everyone and telling everyone. I had to talk to the cops and Children's Aid Society a few more times.

"Court proceedings started eventually. He plead guilty. I had to stand up in court and tell my story. There were so many strangers standing behind me in support. They shouted names at him in the hall. They hugged me, and said how sorry they were.

"I look back now and think these people were not ready to hear this story. I remember looking up from the stand after reading my victim impact statement, and there was not a dry eye. It was so silent. I looked my uncle directly in the eye for the last time and said, 'Now I am free.' But I was far from free. He still controlled me emotionally, for a long time. I went through many phases dealing with everything I endured, similar to the stages of grief. Denial, anger, more anger, regret, and probably more."

Steph's self-esteem was sabotaged by her uncle prior to the roller coaster of teenage insanity, also known as high school. Everything she endured, accompanied by an unhappy home life where she was raised by "not a good mom, who did the best she could" made Steph's turbulent teenage years almost unbearable.

"High school kids suck; they truly suck. I was very suicidal in grade 9. I felt so ashamed of myself and what happened to me. I couldn't deal with the pressure of being a high school student and a rape/abuse victim trying to seek justice from our judicial system.

I never thought I was pretty. I didn't think I was worthy of good things. I didn't think my friends wanted to be my friends, and only stuck around because they felt sorry for me.

"I no longer felt like anyone was on my side. I started cutting my wrists; I don't know why exactly. I don't know if I wanted to die, or that it was an outlet for everything happening. I didn't trust my therapists; everyone was trying to tell me how to feel and act. I was entering a whole new world of being a teenager. I was filled with anger and hatred for many reasons."

Steph eventually found inspiration in a neighbor, Adam, who had spina bifida. In spite of his illness, he was happy; and through Adam, Steph was introduced to other special needs children. She saw so much love, laughter and light within these children, and it lifted her. She went through a dark period when Adam passed away suddenly, leading to self-destructive choices.

"One day I woke up and thought to myself, *Adam wouldn't be happy with me.* I wanted to do him right. He's the reason I am a personal support worker. I even had a tattoo done in his memory. He somehow from the great sky above kicked my butt and motivated me to get back on the right track of things in my life. He's my biggest inspiration in life to do better and help others; he helped me more than he knew."

Steph has been helping others as a proud personal support worker for eleven years, and considers her career to be her greatest accomplishment. She tries her best to lift people up during the toughest moments in their lives, just as Adam's positive perspective lifted her when she needed it most. She now has a loving fiancé who has shown her that she is worthy of love, and lifelong friends who have stuck by her through all of life's twists and turns. Her uncle tried to hold her down, but Steph was determined to rise. She will always be a survivor.

Don't bother drying your eyes; the next story is just as difficult to read, unfortunately. Every experience of sexual abuse or assault is different, and we can learn something new from each one. Sandra has had to survive several assaults, starting with being molested at age twelve. She adored horses, and was thrilled when her mom arranged for her to take care of a pony.

"I absolutely loved horses, but we were never able to afford riding lessons or even own a horse ourselves. This opportunity meant the world to me. There was an older man (maybe in his sixties) who took care of the stables and the horses. He showed me the ropes on how to saddle a horse, how to brush him, scrape his hooves, and of course, how not to get bitten or kicked while doing that."

Every little girl's dream job! That's what it *should* have been, if it wasn't for perverted men taking advantage of their position of power. Something that should have been so special was ruined by the criminal behavior of a person trusted with caring for a child. Sandra eloquently expressed the brutality of his actions and how it impacted her.

"As much as I enjoyed taking care of that pony, I was in love with the big horses. So, when the stable master one day asked if I wanted to ride his horse to get a feel for being on a big one, I was more than willing to go. I remember sitting on this beautiful golden-brown animal while he held the reins and walked beside us.

"It was a beautiful warm summer's day. The air smelled like dust, flowers, grass, and horse. We walked along fenced meadows and a couple of fields until we came to a shed. He said he just had to go inside to get something, and he wanted to give his horse a rest, since it was such a warm day. He helped me down, and we went inside.

"I don't remember much about the interior of the shed, but what I do remember was that there was a bed with a dusty, rough blanket in one corner. I remember that part so vividly because that was where he asked me to sit down. He molested me that day.

"I did not understand why he began to stroke my breasts or tried to touch me between my legs. I had no idea what sexuality meant. I was too young for the sex-talk, and I had not yet been interested in boys. I just knew that it felt wrong."

Sandra didn't know what he was doing or how to respond. Of course, he knew exactly what he was doing. He gained her trust and built a relationship, offered the big horses to get her closer, took her away to a secluded spot to trap her, and touched her knowing it was wrong. He is the only one to blame. Sandra did the only thing she could, which was tell someone after the fact.

"When I came home from the stables that day, I did not know what to do. I didn't know if I should tell anyone. I felt strange. I was worried that my parents would be angry or disappointed in me. I could not make sense of what had happened. Luckily, I told a friend who came by that day, and he insisted that I tell my parents. He even went with me to my mom.

"When I told her, she first just stared at me. Then she said, 'Don't go there anymore!' That was the only time she ever spoke about what had happened to me. She was not prepared for what I had told her."

As mothers and daughters, we can see both sides of that situation. Her mother reacted poorly, unintentionally silencing Sandra. No one wants to be on either side of that conversation. However, it creates lasting issues that can't be ignored. Blocking out the unbearable moments and not reliving them are common survival techniques for those who've faced trauma.

However, you should first tell someone you trust what happened, and have that person reassure you that you're not to blame. If you are courageous enough, the authorities should go after the predator. It will never be easy, but women cannot continue to let this behavior pass as acceptable.

The pattern repeated when a sexually aggressive hotel owner chased her around, trying to touch her breasts. She was only fourteen and her mother brushed it off as men being men. My first boss was a lot like this guy; I was also only fourteen years old when he made inappropriate jokes and advances towards me. Unlike Sandra, I didn't tell any adults until significantly later.

"The owner liked to drink. A *lot*. Drinking wasn't the only bad habit he practiced. He was known for teasingly groping women's breasts. Most female guests knew this about the owner and endured his advances, because no one felt there was any other ulterior motive behind his so-called casually inappropriate advances. He was, more often than not, seen as the drunken hotel owner who liked to fondle women's breasts. His vice was no secret, and no one ever really complained about him, simply because he never did anything more than briefly grope breasts.

"I never expected the owner to come at me that day and actually try to touch my breasts. I was 14 years old. Still an innocent girl, but not naïve. I immediately said *no*, then ran away from him. But my voice was not heard, no matter how many times I said no. My feelings didn't matter. He just kept coming after me, practically chasing me around the hotel. This traumatic ordeal went on for about half an hour, until finally my parents returned. I ran to my mother in tears, telling her what had happened.

"Again, my fear, my shock, my feelings were dismissed. My mother decided to laugh off the entire ordeal. She explained to me that the owner did that to every woman and that he meant no harm. Then, in a joking tone, she told the owner that he couldn't behave inappropriately with her fourteen-year-old daughter, since I did not understand that he was just playing around. I was stunned into silence and grief.

"Once again, my mother had failed me. She had made me feel like a silly, naïve girl for not allowing this lecher to touch my breasts. What I ended up learning yet again that day was that my parents couldn't protect me. And apparently it was not only common, it was completely accepted that a man could touch a woman wherever he wanted, whenever he pleased. Women had no say in the matter."

How many women reading this book can relate to what Sandra just shared?

It resonates with me, and it's not just my mother or her mother. So many women, almost all older women—up until maybe the generation after mine—tend to sweep men's bad behavior under the rug, as if it is something we are expected to endure. *Men are pigs. Men can't help themselves. They think with their dicks.* That's the story we tell ourselves, and each other.

It's time to change that narrative! I want to put a fierce expletive in front of the word narrative because this topic angers me, as I'm sure it does many women. However, I can tell Sandra is a spiritual and peaceful being. This is her chapter, and I won't let my anger over toxic masculinity overshadow her story of triumph.

Of course, the next time Sandra was sexually harassed working at a restaurant, she said nothing. Women learn to accept sexual harassment as a part of being employed in the hospitality industry. Years later, when she was sexually assaulted by a military officer, she screamed "RAPE!" and fought him off. However, she didn't follow through with charges, even though he penetrated her against her will. This is known as conditioning.

"It was after that sexual assault that I began to question and doubt myself. I began to look for reasons why this had happened to me again. Why had I attracted this horrible experience again? Did I not know how to read men? Was I too open and free in my communication with him? Where had I led this guy on?

"So many questions passed through my mind, all of them self-interrogating, almost self-incriminating. This is what victims of sexual assault and abuse do. They look for reasons to blame themselves, because they think it's the only plausible reason why someone would assault them."

I'm hoping that after reading Renee, JJ, Steph and Sandra's heart-wrenching chapters, you'll be experts on recognizing abuse, understanding its impact and know that it's never the victim's fault. The only one to blame is always the abuser or the rapist. No doubts.

Sandra stopped blaming herself eventually and wanted to fight for justice. When she reached out for advice, she was further silenced.

"I decided to confide in my friends and suggested reporting this guy to the military police. And yet again, I was faced with dismissal. My friends laughed it off as ridiculous, and predicted that I would not be vindicated. Nothing would be resolved by my accusing an officer of the military of rape.

"Instead, they said, I should tell them that I had a relationship with him and had found out that he had a wife in the USA. That would spark the MP's interest, since they held marriages in very high regard. Needless to say, I did not go to the police since I was quite discouraged by their advice and disturbed by their suggestion for me to lie to the officials. I sought my dad's opinion and he flat out said to me: 'It is you against the entire U.S. Army. Who do you think is going to win?' So I dropped my desire to press charges, and never again pursued the incident."

When we bury our pain, it festers and grows. It rots and eats at us from the inside.

"My decision to forget the sexual assault happened made me further withdraw from life. I stopped seeing my friends. I felt no desire to dance or socialize. I felt nothing but fear, anxiety, and emptiness. I became more and more overwhelmed by this great need to isolate myself and search for a way to heal my violated mind and body. This sexual assault haunted me for years."

Trauma lingers if you don't deal with it. I'm happy to say Sandra has since dealt with it, and is now using her life experiences to guide those who are dealing with similar pain. She is a reiki master, a TIR (traumatic incident reduction) facilitator, and a certified coach at Rise Above Your Story, helping others heal from trauma. Sandra is also a first-time author of *Journey to your Self: How to Heal From Trauma*. She's an extraordinary example that women can survive anything and come out stronger.

THE POWER OF
PERSPECTIVE

I've known the next impressive woman for longer than anyone in this book, yet I knew the least about her prior to the interview. It wasn't until I received an email listing a shocking number of challenging illnesses, serious injuries, awful heartbreaks, and physically abusive bullying that I realized just how strong she must be.

Carrie was one of the few participants who suggested herself. She sent the email after I posted on Facebook that I was searching for three more women who had an inspiring story of overcoming obstacles. The confidence it took to raise her hand and ask, "What about me?" is a relatively new ability for Carrie. She would ordinarily avoid the attention, out of fear of judgment or rejection.

This time, she bared the hardest moments from her life in a short, scrambled email. Carrie is dyslexic, which has made reading and writing quite challenging throughout her entire life. When she struggled to excel in school, her teachers dismissed it as either a lack of effort or being a slow learner. It wasn't until she was in college that she admitted she reads backwards, then forwards, and had to jumble words together in an attempt to find their meaning.

"You just assume that everyone reads backwards and then forwards. I read very quickly backwards and then very quickly forwards; then I have to put together the words to figure out what it's supposed to say."

Dyslexia is only one of the diagnoses Carrie has been given throughout her life, and she hasn't let it or anything else hold her back. Carrie also has OCD, anxiety, a demyelinating condition, and has suffered from debilitating depression. For Carrie, some challenges she was born with, some developed, some were a side effect of a challenged life, and some were just unbelievably unlucky. Even with her hodgepodge of misfortunes, she created her own success as an ambitious entrepreneur of an award-winning massage therapy clinic.

That's because according to Carrie, she's incredibly lucky. She finds the good in everyone and any situation. Carrie views being caught and almost crushed in a set of elevator doors as a blessing. She recognizes that the accident could have taken her life, and is simply grateful that she survived the painful ordeal.

"I'm not accident prone. I'm blessed. I have an amazing guardian angel who's tired. I think I'm lucky. From researching being caught in an elevator door, you wouldn't believe the decapitations and injuries that happen. It pinned me by the arms and caused nerve damage that impacts my life as a massage therapist. Granted, it is a shitty injury and I still suffer from it, but it could have been a lot worse."

Carrie adapted and developed new techniques due to her injuries, and it motivated her to continuously study anatomy and ways to assist the human body with healing. Carrie is a wealth of knowledge when it comes to anything ailing you, and has personally guided me through several joint and back issues. Her pain has become a tool to help others heal.

What stood out about Carrie sharing her story was the attitude she maintained from one random ordeal to the next unexpected situation. She kept the same cheery outlook when she had just turned forty, then broke her leg in two places after she fell during a five-kilometer walk. Well, she actually only broke it in one spot when she fell; the second break came when the staff at the event carried her down the hill in an ATV. They hit a bump and she heard the break, loud and clear. The damage from that day resulted in four depressing months in a nursing-home style hospital room, being told that she would never walk again. Carrie was informed that she would need to sell her house, because she would be put into a nursing home—indefinitely.

"It was then that I realized people need to be an advocate for themselves. It's why I became a motivational speaker and share my thoughts on the importance of self-care."

Carrie has had to cope with so much emotional and physical pain in her life that it has become easy for her to rise above. She knows how pain feels and uses hers to heal. Carrie could never wish harm on anyone, even those who've wronged her.

Carrie wasn't very popular in grade school and was picked on for simply being herself. Several of her classmates pinned her down and expressed their displeasure in her lack of conformity by attempting to burn her nose with a lighter. They picked on her relentlessly in school, and then tricked her into trusting them.

"I think the reason I'm so nice and always trying to make others happy is because I know how much it sucks to be hurt."

She couldn't understand why her classmates didn't like her, so she naïvely believed they had a change of heart when they invited her to play with them on the climbing bars. During recess, they called her over and suddenly, she was literally hanging out with the cool kids.

"I didn't have a lot of friends in grade school, and I desperately wanted to be popular. They asked me to climb up and play with them."

Kids can be so cruel.

There was an evil plan in motion. The rest of the kids were clinging to the bar tightly, anticipating the next move. One of the bigger kids fiercely shook the tall, metal pole protruding from the sand pit. A few whips of the pole sent Carrie flying from the bar, landing on a very solid railroad tie that framed the pit.

Those bullies injured several of her ribs. An evil, childish, act of bullying hospitalized Carrie. I could tell how the incident still haunted her, as she never really understood why they attacked her. She had never harmed anyone, so it tore at her confidence to wonder why they felt she deserved such a violent response to her mere existence.

It was around thirty years later, and retelling the pain of that moment still provoked genuine tears. It was the first time I saw a crack in her armor, showing signs that some things are a bit harder to just accept and move forward. However, when she encountered the same bullies nearly thirty years later, she kept her head held high.

"They came in and asked for massages, and I gave them the best ones I possibly could. I wanted them to know that I'm a good person, and I didn't want to hold a grudge."

They walked into her massage therapy clinic and didn't recognize her, or at least didn't give any indication that they recalled what they put her through. Maybe they knew, but the traumatic memories of bullying are always more vibrant to the one who was under attack. Her former classmates, knowingly or unknowingly, allowed their bodies to be treated by someone who they had repeatedly bullied.

A combination of Carrie's peaceful, forgiving personality and a desire to show her former bullies that she was a good person allowed her to find a way to swallow the pain from her past and be the skilled, thorough therapist that her business was built on. She gave them the best massage of their lives, and was rightfully proud of how she handled it. Being kind to her bullies gave her a little closure.

Learning how to modify her perspective and find the blessing in any heartbreak was a technique she developed after her fiancé left her with a Dear Jane note—right after she mailed out their wedding invitations. He was her everything; then he was gone, with only a cold, heartbreaking note stating that he had never loved her.

"We were together for three years and he was my world. We never fought. I left my art program at Sheridan College to be with him, switching to graphic design. I walked in the door after mailing the wedding invitations, and sitting on the glass top of our coffee table was a letter saying 'it's over,' and 'I can't help it. I was getting dressed in the morning, listening to *Losing My Religion*, and it made me realize that I don't love you.' He never loved me? I was crushed."

Carrie sacrificed so much for their love yet he could walk away, stating he'd never loved her. She was studying to become a part of his religion. She switched colleges just so they could live in the same city. There were no warning signs, he was just gone.

A groom-to-be skipping out before a wedding is an overwhelming and heartbreaking experience, especially for someone who had battled severe insecurities due to relentless bullies and a learning disability. The confidence she was trying to build since high school was suddenly smashed to pieces.

Her mental health suffered to the extent that she had to drop out of her graphic design program to focus on her well-being. Carrie had a mental breakdown, and needed a physical break with professional care to heal. She shared this with me and allowed me to include it in this book despite her fear of how others would perceive her struggles with mental health.

"I was told to hide what happened because it would affect my future employment, that some may look on it as a weakness."

Carrie is not the only person in this book to admit to mental health issues, or to needing professional help. That's the purpose of this book: sharing our experiences so that we know we're not alone. Everyone struggles, and it doesn't mean you're weak. Rising from those moments is what makes us stronger.

"It was a traumatic experience. Withdrawing failed me out of my course when I was actually passing. Graphic design was something I wanted since I was a little girl. It took years, but that experience ended up becoming a turning point in my life."

She didn't go back into graphic design, venturing into schooling to be a professional support worker instead. Carrie has a sincere desire to help people heal. While she was working as a PSW, patients started requesting her because she would give them little massages to help them relax. One of the patients suggested she pursue massage therapy. Once she looked into it, she was intrigued.

"I didn't realize massage was something I could do as a profession. It's anatomy, which was ideal because I wanted to be a medical illustrator when I was studying art. Discovering massage therapy was more neurology, and pathology piqued my interest; I dove in. I still go back to school to study new techniques so that I will have more to offer my clients."

Carrie worked in the field for a bit before her supportive husband Scott encouraged her to start her own business. Above & Beyond Massage Therapy Clinic has grown, with several therapists joining her; the clinic has earned numerous awards, and soared past the ten-year milestone. She found true love with her awesome husband, and has rescued border collies for twenty years. She has a quiet life with Scott and their dogs, and holds no anger or resentment for everything she had to endure to get here. Carrie could get tossed off a cliff (though she sincerely hopes that this doesn't happen!) and be confident that she will rise again.

I had a kickass woman in mind for the second half of this chapter, but she didn't end up answering my questions. I held her space until the weekend prior to submitting the final draft to my publisher for editing, before finally accepting that her answers were not coming. I could have easily panicked, but my positive perspective helped me realize that this setback was meant to be.

I was already feeling guilty about another local leader who deserved to be in this story. I originally asked her over a year ago and then changed my mind, solely due to the fact she was in the process of writing her own story. Everything about her exemplifies a woman ready to rise. However, I was specifically searching for untold stories.

As you've already read, two of my participants are authors who *are* sharing their story outside of this book. I didn't realize they were in the process of writing a memoir-style book when I asked for their involvement. When I discovered they were authoring expanded versions of their personal stories, it was too late. I understood the depths of what Sandra and Leonora had survived, and both experiences were too powerful to exclude.

I knew Stacey had a remarkable story worth sharing, and that this was my opportunity to make things right. I sent her a message saying, "I need you," explained what had happened, and told her how quickly I would need her to react. Stacey responded the same day: "No problem. I'll work on this."

My friend's helpful, humble email was all I needed to breathe and proceed as planned. Stacey's enthusiastic get 'er done personality assured me she'd send her answers in time, so I was not surprised when her words of wisdom arrived the day she had promised they would.

> "I believe you see me as an inspiration to other women who may be dealing with the same things, someone they can look to as a source of guidance and support. I want to give hope that even the most difficult things can be overcome with a little bit of faith in oneself and the perseverance to see it through."

Stacey's diligent work ethic has been evident throughout her teaching career, which recently earned her the prestigious 2019 Odyssey Award from the University of Windsor. She is currently pursuing her PhD, and her work examining the academic challenges faced by English language students with special needs was published in 2017.

Until I wrote this story, I didn't realize Stacey was also one of the first female RCMP-trained firearms instructors in Canada, and ranked at the top of her training unit as the only female in a group of men. Her credentials and accolades are quite impressive, but that isn't what makes Stacey's story so powerful: It's the perspective she has gained from every mountain she's climbed.

"I know many people who did not have to go through troubled times in order to be kind and decent. Of course, there are those that have been through so much and are better people for it. If given the opportunity now, there is very little I would change from my past. I truly believe I have acquired an understanding about life and love that many people spend their whole lives trying to find.

"I think that people over-complicate things. If you believe the world is a bad place, then that is what you will see, and you will miss out on all the good. I could have let many things in my life impact me negatively; they had the potential to paralyze me, emotionally.

"I don't want to see the world or people that way. I believe people are inherently good, and we're all just trying to figure out where we fit. Perhaps I see the world through rose-colored glasses, but I'm OK with that; anything less would be an incredible waste of the beautiful life I have been given."

Stacey's success comes from staying positive, seeking out solutions, and overcoming obstacles. Those are the reasons she's risen so high from such humble beginnings. Stacey was thrust into adulthood when she was only a teenager, which became a catalyst for a lifetime of caring for others.

"At a very young age, I became the primary caregiver for my mother. She developed a debilitating autoimmune disease, causing her to lose her kidneys. I would go to school, drop her off for her treatments, and pick her up again.

"Quite often, we would have to pull over for her to vomit because she was so nauseous from treatment. It felt like my high school friends' lives were so different from my own. I was dealing with something much bigger than myself, and they were just trying to figure out which jeans to wear to school."

Growing up a bit too fast is something Stacey and I have bonded over, although in her case, she was mature enough to deal with the added responsibilities (unlike myself, only recently dealing with the many mistakes I made along the way). Her mother's sudden illness brought out the selfless mother in Stacey.

"I was very much into theatrics in school. I enjoyed being involved in drama class and plays. I was planning on attending the American Academy of Dramatic Arts in New York. Unfortunately, when my mom got sick, those plans changed. I was compelled to stay by my mother's side and put my dreams on the back burner. I remember my mom saying that if I wanted to go, she would find a way. That was my mom, always thinking of me during her hardest times. I never went. I had a greater purpose to fulfill at home."

Stacey still does so much for her mother, and always will. It's in her nature. She's an active local philanthropist, and a genuine giver. Stacey has witnessed the impact of giving back and the importance of perspective.

"Teaching and volunteering at an orphanage in Africa was an incredible experience that taught me to be grateful for what I have and appreciate what is in front of me, because life could be so much worse. Seeing children run to you with incredible joy because you have a clean bottle of water to give them, and some clothes, was such an eye opener.

"Upon my return I went through moments of depression, which were felt by many of the other people who shared the same experience. The depression was due to guilty feelings for having to leave, and then returning to a first world nation that provides us with clean water, food, and shelter. It was a hard adjustment, full of mixed emotions. Although I couldn't stay, I at least could take back the memories and the lessons I learned there."

As a stellar teacher, Stacey is applying those lessons everywhere she can. When she discovered the lack of a local support group for women dealing with fertility issues, she decided to create one. Stacey's Facebook group, Fertility Friends, offers women dealing with various fertility issues an open platform for discussing their feelings, frustrations, and medical findings.

"As someone who prides themselves on making things happen, this was something I could not control. I was doing everything the doctors told me to do: eating right, exercising, relaxing, praying, meditating, yoga. None of it worked, and each month only led to more heartache.

"That was an incredibly difficult pill to swallow. I was confused, sad, and resentful. I was questioning my faith and looking for deeper meanings. I felt ashamed that I couldn't fix whatever was preventing us from having the family we so deeply wanted. And at that point, I had not shared my story and struggle with others. I felt as if I was living a lie, telling people we just weren't ready for children, or that we weren't trying.

"One month, after trying to conceive for over two years, I was absolutely convinced that I was finally pregnant. It was too early for a pregnancy test, but I was *sure* of it. I ran to the store to buy this onesie that said 'Dad's #1 Quarterback,' as my husband is a huge football fan. I got home, wrapped it up, and put it in a gift bag, then waited for test day to confirm what I felt certain to be true.

"But I was *not* pregnant. My body and mind had tricked me once again, and my heart sunk to a new low. I quickly stuffed the bag into my bottom drawer, where it sat for two more years. The doctors would continue to tell us that there was no medical reason why it wasn't happening, but that only made us feel worse.

"It was a very dark time in my life where I felt isolated. I did not want to leave the house, avoided conversations about anything baby related, and friends with children, while I experienced the deepest despair I've ever known.

"Through it all, my husband was my rock. But even the best of relationships feel the strain and pressure of failing to conceive. Not to mention the negative effects on your body, both emotionally and physically, as a result of aggressive treatments, weight loss, weight gain, mood swings, and exhaustion. So many times, I wanted to give up...but there was something inside that kept pushing me.

"I didn't want to focus on the negativity and loss anymore. I needed to get back to the old me. I felt strongly that finding positive distractions and being of service to others in need would put things in perspective in my own life. Starting two groups brought me back to life emotionally, from a place that felt so lonely and isolating. I'm a go big or go home kind of person, so a few months after I started the groups, I felt compelled to share my truth. And, what better way to do that than on the radio for Infertility Awareness Week, with thousands of Windsorites listening."

Bravo Stacey! What a brave and powerful way to share your story. Stacey provides constant encouragement to those who reach out, and even organizes a monthly meeting at her home. On top of managing the women in her fertility groups, she is also the founder of Women of Windsor, a local women's group that hosts women's empowerment events and gives back to the less fortunate.

"That proved to be the best decision I could have made. I had so many people messaging me with support, but also those looking for support. I felt proud that I had a group that could do just that. I contacted Fertility Matters Canada to notify them that there was not a Southwestern Ontario support group within their services, which led to me becoming the Southwestern Ontario representative for the organization.

"From there things took off, and I returned to my roots in philanthropy while supporting other women who were struggling with their own fertility issues. Ironically, the very day of our first group meeting, I received a call from the clinic saying they had an unexpected spot open up for me on the IVF list, six months early. I really believe when you give selflessly to others, life always gives back to you in some unexpected way."

Stacey continuously gave of herself to everyone else, while hoping with prayer upon prayer that one day her wish of being a mom would be fulfilled. I'm thrilled to say she and her husband were recently blessed with the precious baby girl she had waited so long to hold. When you give of yourself freely, the world gives back. Thank you, Stacey, for coming to my rescue and sharing your story with us.

PAYING IT FORWARD

I hounded the next warrior woman for well over a year, because having her in this story was a necessity. Natalie (a member of the women's group I mentioned earlier, but not its founder named Natalie) is a very busy entrepreneur. Like many other participants, she was battling her own worthiness when it came to being a part of this book. I already knew bits and pieces of what she had gone through from private conversations we've shared, and have been in awe of her resilience ever since.

I kept asking Natalie for her involvement because of the uniqueness of what she's experienced and how high she's risen from it. Fortunately, she finally had the courage to pour out her heart into a series of emotional voice clips. She didn't hold anything back, because she truly understands the impact her story can have on other women. Later she shared with me the therapeutic power of expelling her life story into these raw, two-minute outpourings. It was a realization she came to somewhere in the middle of giving her answers.

> "That's the purpose of the book. The more raw and authentic you are, the better yield and more help it will create for other people."

All of her answers centered on how her experiences could help those who are struggling; a common trait found in many of the women in this story. Natalie had a tough childhood, often feeling unsupported by her parents. Her trauma was compounded by being raped and abused, then needing to hide out in a women's shelter. Natalie knows firsthand how meaningful it is to have strangers support you when you feel all alone and hopeless.

"You really find your true self when you walk through fire. I found my calling and my true passion from some of the worst experiences in my life. My son was a result of a sexual assault, so he has no one but me. During the pregnancy, it was a really dark time. Thankfully, through that fire became a beautiful thing: my son, my sweetheart."

Natalie's children are her world, and she continues to rise in spite of intense injuries, destructive relationships and countless challenges. She's the CEO of a global romance enhancement direct sales business, Femme Fatale Parties Inc., which employs and empowers women. She creates her own line of products, negotiates with factories overseas, and is constantly reinventing ways to grow the business. Natalie's well known locally for her charitable efforts, including raising the funds to buy 200 sleeping bags for the homeless and co-hosting a beautiful gala with Stacey from the previous chapter, that raised $5,500 for the Hiatus House.

"I'm proud that my kids want to help me feed the homeless or hand out sleeping bags. I'm proud that I'm instilling that value, the mindset of gratefulness and serving others, in my children. I want my legacy to be something I contribute to the world, and my sons and daughter will carry that mission forward."

It's not only her children who have been influenced by her efforts. I attended her event this year to hand out sleeping bags, and was forever touched by the experience; I'm certain I wasn't the only one. A mutual friend Donna, with a heart of gold, was there volunteering for the second year in a row. She told me that she had brought her best friend with her because of the impact it had on her the year prior.

There is an overwhelming feeling of gratitude that pours over you when you give back to those who truly need it. I know that I, Donna, and the countless people I've shared my experience with will show up next year to help. This all began with Natalie.

Philanthropy has been a major part of Natalie's life since she was a young girl. She sponsored underprivileged families and was heavily involved in fundraising throughout her military career. Her passion grew when the Hiatus House took her in when she left the military and an abusive relationship.

> "Hiatus House stepped up in a big way for me and in that support, it opened up my eyes to the needs of others and gave me a sense of community."

The main goal of her business and philanthropy is to give women independence and a sense of community, even if it hurts her margins. That was what was missing in her life when she was a kid. There once was a time she thought the military would give her the support she desperately needed; sadly, she was mistaken. Natalie had ambitious plans to climb the ranks and secure her own financial security.

> "I joined the military thinking it would be a safe haven, compared to the instability I had growing up. I thought I would have community and support. Instead, we become so brainwashed that you don't even defend yourself."

There is no part of me that would sacrifice my personal freedom to serve my country. I respect and admire Natalie's decision to live a challenging life with a noble purpose, but I wouldn't do it, despite sharing in Natalie's, stubborn insistence that she's as tough as any man. After listening to what she endured, there is no way in hell I would have lasted even a week. Natalie is certainly more stubborn than I am.

> "I was a tomboy, and insisted on proving that girls can do anything boys can do. I wanted to be a football player, a police officer, or join the military."

Natalie was in phenomenal physical condition at the time; although basic training was intense, she received the top athlete award, out of 108 people—most of them men. She had what it took to kick ass and prove she was just as strong.

"The military is like a cult. You are constantly put through strenuous shit, testing your physical strength while beating away at your mental willpower. They force you to conform. You can't complain or stop, no matter how bad you hurt. If you can't get out of bed due to pain or illness, they will consider you AWOL and you'll be sent to prison."

That's not even the worst of it. Her master seaman would rub his genitals on her shoulder while she was taking a test, but she couldn't say anything. In her military career, she dislocated her shoulder, had cracked, bleeding feet from trekking through rough terrain, and fell down a flight of stairs with her full gear on. Natalie also miscarried at two months, despite telling her superior that she couldn't handle the drills due to her previous injuries and back problems. None of this mattered to her commanders.

"The military treats you like a machine. When I told my master seaman that I couldn't handle it, he responded, 'If other pregnant women can do it, why can't you?' My previous injuries and pain didn't matter to him."

She lost her sense of self in the military. Natalie thought she had to sit down and take it, knowing in her heart that it wasn't right. That influence drained her prior self-esteem, making her a prime target for abuse. The military put her in a situation where rape is far too common, and speaking up for yourself is not tolerated. When she was honorably discharged, she was recovering in a wheelchair with permanent cartilage damage to her spine, and the overwhelming feeling that she wanted to give up.

This is a lesson I've recently learned, as well. I insisted on lifting objects that were too heavy for me at my day job, instead of asking for help. I did not want to appear weak and ended up damaging my shoulder muscle. The impact that being in pain had on my life truly stuck with me, as I'm sure it did with Natalie.

Women are just as capable as men, but we are not built the same. Most men have greater physical strength than most women, a sad but true fact of nature. Instead of trying to prove our muscles are just as powerful as men's, we need to showcase how our minds are able to compensate for any physical shortcomings. It is brains over brawn, ladies. That is why we can do anything a man can do.

Although she struggled financially and emotionally for years after leaving the military, Natalie has rebounded higher than imaginable. This bombshell beauty was just selected to be Ms. Galaxy Windsor, an honor she was certainly not expecting, but definitely deserves.

Natalie has a lot she could boast about, but her 45 minutes of voice clips were humble and filled with sincerely helpful advice for whoever reads this book. The first accomplishment she listed was her own survival, along with a confession that her real inspiration for living is her three kids.

> "I'm proud that I'm still alive. I tried to overdose a couple of times, but I'm still here. I have dark days and want to give up, but I'm still here."

When she talks about her business, her focus is on giving the women who work for her a home-based, flexible job that can provide financial independence. She offers her employees training, benefits, and marketing assistance beyond typical direct sales opportunities.

> "Femme Fatale Parties gave an avenue for women in Canada and the United States to become financially independent. I invest in my sales reps and offer more than most direct sales companies, because I want more women to become strong and self-reliant."

Do you see now why I chased Natalie for so long? All of the women in this book are equally as impressive, but not many women I know would be crazy enough to join the military, determined enough to stick it out in spite of physical and mental abuse, hit rock bottom with a resounding thud, and then rise so high she's running a global company that literally puts women's personal satisfaction and success into their own hands! Plus, I'm a huge fan of masturbation, especially quality toys. It's no surprise why I adore Natalie and had to have her in my book.

Natalie is an unstoppable woman who has been knocked down too many times to mention. Fortunately, with each blow, she rises stronger and more determined to be a voice for anyone who is struggling.

> "I want to show other women that they are in control of their lives and have the ability to achieve their dreams."

I adore Natalie for her enthusiasm when it comes to paying it forward, which brings me to the 23rd woman I'd like to celebrate in this book. I only interviewed 22 women, and when I decided Kimberly required an entire chapter, it left me with an uneven number of participants. (This was before the last participant dropped out and I sweet talked Stacey into jumping on board at the last minute.)

I knew of another warrior woman with a story comparable to Natalie's. I didn't originally ask her because her life story is already a best-selling book entitled *The Queen's Daughter*, and I was searching for fresh content. Melissa is a friend, a mentor, and an exceptional example of turning the most traumatic moment in your life into a lifetime of paying it forward. She's earned every tribute she gets.

I won't go into the heartbreaking details of what she endured back in 1976, when she was only nineteen years old. You can read everything she experienced in her first book, which is aptly framed in the Amazon description.

> "Kidnapped, beaten, and gang raped at gunpoint. Wanting to die. Begging her assailants to kill her. This is the story of Melissa McCormick: the riveting story of her escape, the night she became The Queen's Daughter."

It's a raw, emotional story that personifies every woman's worst nightmare. I've read it several times to remind me that women have the strength to overcome anything. Melissa didn't just get through the repeated gang rape and death threats on that fateful evening so long ago; she had the smarts to convince her attackers to let her escape. Courageously, she immediately went to the police, despite promising her assailants she wouldn't. Melissa also showed up at the trial for each man involved in the rape to ensure justice was served. Now she uses her experiences to help others deal with the emotional turmoil that follows being sexually violated.

Her full-time career and life purpose is counseling victims of sexual assault. Her registered non-profit, The Queen's Daughter Cause Fund, raises enough money to support Melissa's humble lifestyle, so she can spend her time listening and supporting survivors all over the community. She's a passionate public speaker and promotes open, real dialogue on an issue that is usually kept hidden.

Melissa has filled a variety of roles in her pursuit of lifting survivors, including being president of the Windsor and Essex County Sexual Assault Crisis Center, Windsor Women's Economic Forum, and Ladies' Exclusive Alliance. Melissa has also held various roles for countless charities, and has earned too many awards to list for her work in the nonprofit sector—and that was before making her advocacy work a full-time commitment.

At the end of 2005, Melissa closed her successful retail store after twenty years of business to devote herself fully to the Cause. Her life is now a selfless one that I'm certain I could never manage. I deal with victims of abuse on a small scale, consisting of a few informal chats per month through social media. It feels incredible to help someone when they are struggling, but it can become emotionally draining quite quickly.

Every day, Melissa listens to painful details that have the potential to trigger memories of being gang raped. The impact she knows she's having on others is all the motivation she needs to keep going.

Melissa spends all of her free time coming up with ways to fundraise a basic income so that she has the resources to help as many people as possible. One of her ideas that I think is super cool is creating warrior bracelets. She requests donations of beads and bracelet making supplies, to serve two purposes. The first purpose is to give the survivor something to work on during their counseling sessions. Putting together the bracelets is a therapeutic distraction during difficult conversations.

In return, Melissa sells the bracelets they make for a ridiculously affordable $5.00 (Canadian funds), to raise more money for the Queen's Daughter Cause Fund. This gives victims an opportunity to fund their own healing efforts. It's brilliant, admirable, and proof that she deserves to be included as one of the women ready to rise. Melissa is the voice for victims who do not yet have the courage to stand on their own and speak out against their attackers.

Although I didn't actually interview her and sent her what I wrote as a surprise, I was certain Melissa would agree to let me include her in this story. She knows there is power in sharing painful experiences, and showing those still struggling that they are not alone.

Unfortunately, since Melissa was a woman I decided to squeeze into the story at the last minute, I don't have any direct quotes from her. Thankfully, you can find her words of wisdom almost anywhere online. If you follow her social media platforms and like Melissa's inspirational YouTube channel, you'll quickly see just how much good this powerhouse is putting back into the world.

IF I CAN, SO CAN YOU

This book is packed with real-life examples of how to overcome experiences that could easily destroy a person. Every woman in this book found a way to rise in spite of challenging circumstances or gut-wrenching heartbreak. They are undeniable proof that there's a resilient fighter inside each of us.

We can learn from and be inspired by one another; that's the power of sharing our stories. I'm still learning. I proudly claim to be uncoachable. I don't allow outside influences to infect my creative process and I trust my own instincts, especially in regards to my author career. That doesn't mean I am not continuously finding inspiration in the actions of others.

Throughout the two years that it took me to write this book, my personal life encountered its share of hurdles. Every time I felt frustrated and ready to scream, I opened my Word document and read a few of these triumphant stories. My daily stresses seemed insignificant, compared to what these women have conquered. Their resilience and strength reminds me that I'm also a badass who has risen more times than she can count. Nothing can hold me down for long.

I'm reassured that I'll be OK just by reading what these women have accomplished in spite of every obstacle they've faced. I may have my own way of doing things, but I genuinely love being surrounded by strong, ambitious women. They motivate me to keep pursuing my own path, and to shoot for the stars.

Inspiration is everywhere, and I soak it up like sunshine. I attended an Amplify Your Impact Women's Conference in October as a vendor, and immediately raced home to write this chapter about the power of using your life to have a positive impact on someone else's.

The creator of the conference, whom I briefly mentioned at the beginning of this story, fueled me. She's *amazing.* I'm deeply, sincerely, impressed by my friend Jessica. She is a risen woman who keeps climbing higher.

Although her life has had its share of challenges, I didn't ask her to be a woman in my story. I don't know enough about what she's been through, only that every strong woman I know has gained her strength through hardships. I'm guessing Jessica has fought her way up her share of mountains, and that's why she stands so tall now.

I brought her name up at the beginning of the book, because she recommended Katelynn as a woman ready to rise. She runs a monthly women's empowerment social group (among other things I'll expand on later), and suggested several incredible candidates for this story. That's what Jessica does. She connects and elevates women through their stories.

That's just the tip of the iceberg for this powerhouse. A year ago, she was inspired by a group of leading women at a conference, and wanted to host a similar event in our hometown that would teach women to believe in themselves and follow their hearts. She was so thrilled by the potential of her idea that she signed a contract with the most luxurious rental space in our small, humble city for a big chunk of money.

When I first spoke with her about her event, my heart sank into my stomach. I saw the beauty in her vision, but my money-rationalizing, cheapo self jumped straight to the risk of losing her investment. How many women in our city would invest that kind of money on themselves?

Another local influencer had hosted a two-day women's conference the year prior, and admitted publicly that it wasn't profitable. I love Jessica, and I want to support anything she does, but even I was fighting whether I was willing to part with any of my hard-earned savings to partake in it.

I didn't share my doubts with her and supported her efforts, hoping she could achieve such a feat. I wanted her to prove to me that it was possible. I do big things in a small way, and I'm hesitant to invest large sums on self-promotion. Right now, my focus is on putting every bit extra into retirement savings. My plan is to continue slow and steady growth until I can retire from my day job at fifty, and pursue my author career full time.

Jessica fucking rocked it.

She realized that she'd laid her wallet on the line in a big way, and had to follow through. There were over 100 people in attendance, and it was successful from both an emotional and profitability standpoint. She pulled out all the stops, and her guests were lifted as a result of her efforts. Jessica took the inspiration she received from the conference she attended and spread it to a new group of women. That's what women need, and it's why I wrote this book.

I knew Jessica's women's conference was going to be a success the week prior to the event, when I met with her to drop off a few books for her VIP swag bags. Following her progress from the sidelines, as she took this nugget of inspiration and grew it into a tidal wave, definitely impacted me. She motivated me to spend a few hundred dollars on bookmarks with my logo and website, and to pick a bigger location for the launch celebration of *Women Ready to Rise*.

Since she opened my eyes, I'm loosening the purse strings a bit when it comes to self-promotion. I just spent $200 on a book promotion service for *Her Own Hero* that launches next week. If it's successful, I'll do the same for *Women Ready to Rise*.

There are no guarantees when you invest in yourself. My Aunt Liz lent me the money for my first 250 copies of *Dark Confessions of an Extraordinary, Ordinary Woman* because she believed in me enough to invest, and I paid her back as soon as I was profitable. Someone else took a chance on me; now it's time for me to do the same.

Jessica believed in herself and went for it in a big way. She's extraordinary, but also just as ordinary as you and I. Every woman in this book has had a moment where life felt impossible, yet they pushed through and rose above the pressure. If they can, so can you.

As part of my interview process, I asked each of the warrior women what advice they would give to anyone who is facing similar struggles or feelings of hopelessness. Their answers were so brilliant and powerful! I gathered all of them together to give every reader reassurance that if they can do it, so can you.

Katelynn, who survived the worst of foster care and losing a child, reminds us that we're not in this world alone.

"Ask for help. Don't be ashamed to say 'I don't know,' or 'I can't do this alone.' Follow the fear. If there is a dream you have, are you scared or excited? GO FOR IT!! That's a huge sign that you're on the right path!"

Kim's words of wisdom are:

"Appreciate love if you have it, because love is a gift that many people don't get to experience."

Proud teen mom Cathy offers realistic hope.

"It doesn't get easier, it gets better. No way would I have predicted I would be a forty-year-old divorcee with two adult children, a mortgage, debt, and broken relationships. I wouldn't change it; I would still have my son, I would still fight for him, I would still dredge through the education system in spite of the social expectations. I would still find a way. I realize that my life isn't easy, but it's good. It's getting even better."

Deb dealt with losing both her parents and becoming a parent herself before the age of nineteen.

"I think it's important for every woman to understand in her heart of hearts that no bad situation will last forever. The past has passed, and the future holds endless possibilities. There is a lesson to learn from absolutely everything that comes your way, and the not-so-great obstacles we face are the most valuable ones. They teach us forgiveness, compassion, empathy, and kindness. They show us what we *don't* want, and they motivate us towards continuous improvement. They build us up and make us stronger."

Kimberly discovered just how strong she could be when Liam was born, so please trust her advice:

"Don't give up. You're capable of more than you realize. Network with those with similar struggles, educate yourself, and don't allow anyone to place limits on what you can do."

TEDx speaker Coach Tina tells it like it is.

"If you want more with your life, you are the only one that can create that. Your choices. Look inside yourself; the answers are there. Once you choose to deal with whatever is keeping you stuck, don't be afraid of the change. Everything you want is on the other side of your fear."

Lisa says this:

"Emotions are real, but we were never taught how to feel. And everyone feels emotions differently. There's no right or wrong way to feel, but when you talk about your emotions, you realize everyone around you is struggling or has struggled."

Dana knows that her hardest moments created the strong woman she is today.

"We do not learn without mistakes and lessons. There is a reason things turn out the way they do. When I am asked what I would say to my younger self or if I can give my younger self advice, I say not a damn thing. You have to go through what you go through sometimes to get to where you are meant to be or need to be. I would not be who I am if not for my challenges. I am grateful for that."

Nurse Kenzie's life has taught her countless lessons.

"I see people day in and day out who are experiencing similar events finding the support they need. They find hope. Don't give up, because there is so much more out there. People do desperate things, and are faced with difficult decisions everyday. It's about how we process them and think of the future, even if we don't think there is one. There is always a future, and you can overcome the thoughts and negativity. Sometimes we just need help. Push the pride aside and ask. You may be embarrassed, but everyone has gone through struggles of some kind. One day, you may even be asked to help."

Sheryl's advice is to look within to find the answers you need, and never give up.

"Change what is making you uneasy or unhappy. Find a sympathetic and trusting ear. Have a mentor. Network. Be in the community. When you verbalize your thoughts, the answers are there. You have to listen to your heart and know that the truth is always in front of you. Then, act on your truth."

Rahel passionately states,

"Don't give up!! *Ever*!! No matter what type of problem you are facing in life, whether it is personal, financial or work-related, you can and will get over the issue. We tend to get so wrapped up in our problems that they seem monumental, and become something we fear we can never escape or fix. You can figure out a way, even if it takes a few tries."

Cancer survivor Leonora encourages you to...

"Never give up, because there is only one you, and you are not replaceable. Take every fear, pain, and hurt and throw it all back with your vibrant and positive and beautiful self! Too many times I see women who are struggling—let it go! It is so easy to focus on negativity; we need to shift our minds' way of thinking, and be hopeful, inspired, and positive—even when you feel at times it may feel hopeless! Thank goodness there is tomorrow. Make every day count! You are special, and unique. You are YOU!"

She may be legally blind, but her vision for life is 20/20. Evie reminds us to...

"Never ever give up. You have so much inside of you that is beyond value. Your thoughts do not have to control your choices. Meditate. Do your work. Love yourself. You can do anything. *Trust the process.* And do your dishes."

Jenny shares her methods for taking control of her thoughts.

"Start with your breath and slow things down. Anxiety for me is a rush; it's a whirlwind. Like uncontrolled freefall and a parachute that won't open. Chaos and lies in my head. *Noise.* What if, what if, WHAT IF? I find my truth when I remember to breathe. This is something I am still learning and practicing."

Mental health advocate Jody gives this passionate advice:

"First off, please reach out. Whether it be a friend, family member, stranger, or on social media, you will be shocked at the number of hands that reach back. As much as you feel alone in your thoughts, there are thousands of people experiencing similar emotions. When things get too overwhelming, try breaking the weeks down into days, the days down into hours, and if need be, the hours into minutes. You will be surprised how many minutes you can make it through...and before you know it, you have survived another day. Life is not about the big things; it is primarily composed of small things, sights, sounds, smells, gestures etc. Try to hold onto the little things instead of always grasping for the big things; the little things keep us going. When we put pressure on ourselves with big life goals and we don't achieve them in the 'right' amount of time, or at all, we call ourselves failures. Instead of assigning ourselves such large tasks, break them down into small, achievable goals. Accomplishing small goals builds confidence."

Renee wants to remind the reader, and herself, to keep going.

"Don't give up. There will be setbacks, and that's OK. Don't let fear stop you; let it *motivate* you. Create your support network and use it. You are not alone!"

JJ admits the biggest problem with her plan to leave her abusive marriage was not telling someone she trusted what was going on.

"Tell someone! You're not alone. I cannot express this enough. Make baby steps, but tell someone. You will feel like the weight of the world has been lifted from your shoulders if you just speak to one person who gets it. Also, set an example for your child(ren). *Be* the example, regardless of whether you have sons or daughters. Deal with your shit—or you will never truly get past it. Show them what a strong woman looks like, regardless of education, language, religion, orientation, or financial resources. Fight like a mother to your last breath."

Strong survivor Steph knows some wounds take longer to heal.

"My advice for women struggling is to be prepared. It's a long road to overcoming our tragedies. It's OK to ask for help. It's OK if you have to take medication from a doctor to help you cope and get through it. If a doctor or counselor is not working for you, then drop them like a hot potato and find one who does help. There is no set time to heal. Time and forgiveness will make it better. I had to forgive my abuser to move on. I will never forget, but I personally had to forgive. If you're someone who has not come forward, it's never too late to tell; it's never too late to seek justice from those who have wronged you. Tell your story; you will never know who it can inspire."

Sandra quotes perhaps the most legendary woman ready to rise.

"Oprah once said, 'Turn your wounds into wisdom.' Those were the words that inspired me to rise above my past and use it to help others. We all have our past, our traumas, our losses, our downfalls, and our failures. Yet each and every one of these experiences teach us, shape us, help us grow...if we allow it. I chose not to let my past control my future. I chose to leave my past behind, and move forward with the knowledge I gained from my healing journey. Trauma can be terrifying until we realize that we are always in control of whether we allow it to control our lives or not. No matter what happens, we can always choose to get our control back and move into a brighter tomorrow."

Stacey offers this reminder:

"Never give up, no matter what it is you're going through or trying to overcome. Dark days will come, but so soon will the light. Allow yourself to grieve; loss comes in many forms. Allow yourself to feel angry or to cry, just don't stay in that place forever. Always listen to your gut, but lead with your heart—and know that while it may not happen right away, this too shall pass."

Carrie's advice to anyone going through similar challenges is this:
"Own it, learn from it and move on. Everyone is going through something. Don't dwell on it. Turn the page and keep going."

Natalie knows you have to trust yourself.
"Silence the noise of others around you. Be true to yourself, listen to your own voice, and have the courage to say no. You will never please everyone."

The reasons I decided to group all of this practical and powerful advice into one chapter was to highlight the similarities. Very few of these women know each other, and the hardships they went through were quite different. In spite of their original life experiences, their advice is basically the same. No matter how bad things feel at the moment, never give up. It will get easier. You will get through it.

Their answers were the same, because it's true.

If they can do it, so can you.

WE WILL RISE AGAIN

After reading all of these awe-inspiring stories of survival, it's easy to see why I'm so successful. I'm surrounded and supported by so many strong women. I see what they are able to overcome and accomplish, reminding me that anything is possible.

This book is also proof that regardless of our personal pain and individual struggles, we are not alone. Someone else has felt the same way, or still feels the same way. Someone has survived what you're going through.

What you just read is only a small sampling of the women I've encountered; everyone I know has a story worthy of being in this book. Think of everyone in your life and everything they've overcome. Human beings are incredibly resilient. We may get knocked down a time or two, but we find the strength to stand back up.

It's pushing through the moments, when it feels like it would be easier to give up, that shows us just how strong we can be. As a survivor of abuse, it took living through the pain of rock bottom to realize that I had the power to handle whatever life throws my way. It gave me confidence and faith that I will always carry with me, challenge after challenge. Every woman in this book, and everyone reading it, should feel that same reassurance.

Even if it feels tragically hopeless in the moment, you have to believe that it will eventually get better. Surviving something that should have killed you gives you a new super power. Whether you conquered abuse, rape, cancer, loss, an accident, addiction, trauma, or tragedy, it gives you this resilient feeling that you will bounce back again. Each hardship makes it oddly easier to get through the next.

You don't fear or stress. You don't let little things get to you. You stand tall, knowing that you'll find a way to deal and move forward. You bounce back up sometimes before anyone has the chance to knock you down.

You're a survivor. Surviving is what you do.

It's like anything in life: The more you conquer, the more capable you become. When you reach the point that negativity doesn't phase you, and you feel confident going into a crisis, then it's time to pay it forward. You were most likely helped along your way back up, and now you can extend your hand to those needing a lift.

It can be something simple, vulnerable, and empowering, like sharing your stories with others who may be lacking hope or in need of guidance. It could be listening and holding space for another who needs to be heard and validated. Big or small, the power of kindness comes from it being contagious. When we reach out to help someone, it inspires them to pass it on.

I'm absolutely honored that Katelynn, Kim, Cathy, Deb, Kimberly, Tina, Lisa, Dana, Kenzie, Sheryl, Rahel, Leonora, Evie, Jenny, Jody, Renee, JJ, Steph, Sandra, Carrie, Stacey, and Natalie trusted me to capture their stories, and allowed me to share them with each of you. I know the courage it takes to put yourself out there, as well as the positive influence stories like theirs will create.

Four of the women had to use aliases to protect themselves from retaliation over the details they shared. In spite of their genuine fears, they knew their stories had powerful potential. They understood the impact their experiences will have on someone going through something similar, and used that as their inspiration.

Several of these women admitted that they had confessed a part of their story that was previously untold, even to those people in their lives who are closest to them. Getting it off of their chest was therapeutic and empowering.

I took my responsibility as the narrator seriously, and left as much as I could in their own words. I gave control over to each woman, messaging back and forth until we were certain it captured everything that mattered, authentically. I allowed participants to make changes I would not have done on my own. The two most common changes requested were to either remove something flattering about themselves, or remove something unflattering about someone else.

Even these fierce fighters have a hard time complimenting themselves or celebrating their strengths; I had to subtly sneak it in where I could. They didn't want to trash their lazy exes or blame anyone who caused them any pain. Their focus was on how they rose and who could be lifted by hearing their story.

I share those urges and fight past them. When Chelsea Girard sent me her over-the-top, highly-flattering-to-me review of this book, I wanted to cut out a few sentences. I was humbled and felt unworthy, but forced myself to follow through with the review in its entirety. Deep down, I know I've earned her praise.

Prior to publishing, I was working on obtaining content approval from each woman and sent Katelynn a quote I planned on adding to her nearly-finished story. In her response, she stated, "I can only imagine how emotionally taxing this book has been to write."

Her words made me think. I may have cried my share of tears writing these highly emotional experiences, but each one raised my spirits in the end. Ultimately, it hasn't been draining or taxing; their stories are *fuel*. It all reminds me that no pain is too great to hold me down for long. Every woman in this book is undeniable proof of the resilience and fortitude of the human spirit.

I hope you will take these powerful little words of reassurance to heart:

We are all *Women Ready to Rise*.

RISE, RISE AGAIN

Jenn Sadai

Reach, extend, stretch towards the surface.
Push, pull, fight your way to solid ground.
Any being can fall into a deep dark place.
Every soul has the inner strength to rebound.

Pray, hope, shout out, loud enough to be heard.
Lift your chin in the direction you're headed.
Take hands of loved ones who are concerned.
Stay still and sink, or stand and ascend it.

Believe, trust, find faith this hole is not permanent.
Feel the light up above, showing you the way to go.
Every struggle strengthens us; that's the true intent.
Each knock down grants us a chance to grow.

Climb up with vigor; let your triumph fuel you higher.
Building muscles, resilience, confidence with each step.
An internal burning ember will rise from this damn fire.
A new invincibility, no challenge you can't accept.

Rise today, rise tomorrow, any day, every day.
No matter the heartbreak, life will not end.
You're a warrior ready for anything sent your way.
You may still fall, but you will rise, rise again.

ACKNOWLEDGMENTS

I feel like the luckiest woman alive for the overwhelming support I receive as an author from too many people to ever possibly list. I wouldn't have accomplished any of this without the encouragement of Rob Sadai, Christine Boakes, Liz Cormier, Jeremy Boakes, Shawna Boakes, Rahel Levesque, Kim Harrison, Deb Birchard, Bill Birchard, Sarah Pinsonneault, Kim Chapieski, Louise Smith, Natalie Hartleib, and Michelle Dupuis. I'm always grateful for the stunning cover design and layout by my forever friend Kim Harrison, and the team at Jan-Carol Publishing, Inc.

JENN SADAI has combined her love of writing with her passion for empowering women into three purposeful series. *The Self-esteem Series* currently contains three non-fiction stories tackling common issues that affect a woman's self-esteem.

Dark Confessions of an Extraordinary, Ordinary Woman explores the dark consequences of domestic violence, drug use, and depression. *Dirty Secrets of the World's Worst Employee* addresses bullying and sexual harassment in the workplace. *Cottage Cheese Thighs* delves into how societal expectations and marketing ploys harm our body image.

The Survivor Series, Her Own Hero and *Her Beauty Burns*, are action-packed, suspenseful fictional stories proving that women have the power to save themselves. Sadai's *True Tales Series* unintentionally began with *No Kids Required*, the true stories of 20 trailblazing women who've chosen not to have children. *Women Ready to Rise* expanded the series, showcasing 22 inspirational stories of turning tragedies into triumphs.

Jenn Sadai is a proud Canadian, born in Windsor, Ontario, where she resides with her heroic husband and two lovable labs. Jenn can always be reached through the various social media links on her website, www.jennsadai.com.

COMING SOON

Jenn Sadai is currently working on the third book in her fictional *Survivor Series, Her Elaborate Escape* as well as an epic, futuristic story she's yet to officially name. She plans on releasing at least one book per year for as long as she can.

CPSIA information can be obtained
at www.ICGtesting.com
Printed in the USA
LVHW041132050420
652183LV00001B/1